GRAMMAR

BEAN

3

지은이	NE능률 영어교육연구소
선임연구원	김지현
연구원	이지영 차연경
영문 교열	Nathaniel Galletta August Niederhaus
디자인	박정진 오솔길 김명진
내지 일러스트	정경호
내지 사진	www.shutterstock.com
맥편집	김선희

GRAMMAR

BEAN

정답 및 해설 3

UNIT 01 will, be going to

B 저는 내일 당신에게 전화할 거예요.
우리는 이번 주말에 캠핑을 갈 거예요.
그녀는 내년에 14살이 될 거예요.
그들은 곧 버스 정류장을 떠날 거예요.

C 저는 책을 읽을 거예요.
우리는 오늘 밤에 춤을 출 거예요.
그녀는 방과 후에 야구를 할 예정이에요.

Mini Grammar

내가 당신을 도와줄게요.
당신은 학교에 갈 거예요.
그는 곧 TV를 볼 거예요.
그녀는 좋은 교사가 될 거예요.
내일은 더울 거예요.
우리는 교실을 청소할 거예요.
그들은 다음 주에 우리를 방문할 거예요.

My Grammar Notes p.9

2. (1) will, will (2) going to, going to

Step1 Warm-Up p.10-11

A 1, 2, 5, 6, 8

B 1. ⓒ, ⓑ, ⓐ 2. ⓑ, ⓐ, ⓒ 3. ⓒ, ⓐ, ⓑ

C 1. It√snow 2. They√go 3. She√be
4. shop√open 5. We√travel
6. He√go 7. There√be 8. I√see

D 1. am going to 2. is going to
3. are going to 4. is going to
5. are going to 6. are going to
7. is going to 8. are going to

Step2 Practice p.12-15

A 1. rain 2. help 3. send 4. make
5. going to 6. be 7. drink 8. attend

B 1. It'll 2. You'll 3. I'm going to
4. He's going to 5. She'll
6. We're going to 7. He'll
8. They're going to

C 1. will be 2. will be 3. is, will be
4. am, will be 5. is, will be
6. was, will be 7. are, will be

D 1. am going to turn 2. are going to be
3. am going to have
4. am going to take 5. is going to dye
6. is going to hit

E 1. will close 2. will pass 3. will meet
4. will drink 5. will go 6. will be

F 1. is going to buy 2. is going to read
3. is going to make 4. is going to fly
5. am going to sell
6. are going to exercise

G 1. will be 2. will get 3. are
4. will take 5. will be 6. go
7. will be 8. will buy
9. will be[is going to be] 10. am going
11. going to play 12. going to
13. to read 14. are going to
15. going to wear 16. to sleep
17. going to give 18. are going

Step3 Grammar into Writing p.16-17

A 1. is going to have, is going to do
2. is going to meet, are going to go
3. is going to exercise, is going to write

4. is going to have a party, is going to stay up

B 1. 1) leave
2) He is going to arrive at 2 p.m.
2. 1) win 2) You will pass the test.
3. 1) rain 2) It will snow this Christmas.
4. 1) are, miss
2) Hurry up! We are going to be late.

C Brian will go to Jeju Island next month. He will climb Halla Mountain on the first day. On the next day, he will try horseback riding. On the last day, he will visit a market for local food.

Wrap-Up Test

p.18-20

1. ③ 2. ① 3. ① 4. ③ 5. ② 6. ② 7. ③ 8. ⑤ 9. ② 10. ⑤ 11. ① 12. are going to 13. closes → close 14. ③ → ① → ② 15. I am going to make Christmas cards

1. be going to는 '~할 예정이다'라는 뜻이다. 주어가 복수이므로 be동사 자리에 are를 쓴다.
2. will 다음에는 동사원형을 쓴다.
3. will은 동사원형 앞에 쓴다.
4. 미래의 결심을 나타내므로 '주어+will+동사원형'의 어순을 취한다.
5. ② will 다음에는 동사원형을 쓴다.
6. now는 현재시제와 함께 쓰고, next year는 미래시제와 함께 쓴다.
7. ①②④⑤ 미래를 나타내는 be going to, ③ 현재 진행 중인 일을 나타내는 현재진행형
8. 미래를 나타내는 be going to와 will은 함께 쓰지 않는다.
⑤ will be going to snow → will snow 또는 is going to snow
9. ② last night(지난밤)은 과거를 나타내므로, 미래시제와 함께 쓸 수 없다.
10. ① am going see → am going to see 또는 will see
② starts → start ③ has → have
④ will going to be → will be 또는 are going to be
11. ① be, ②③④⑤ is
12. next week은 미래를 나타내므로, 'be going to+동사원형'의 어순을 취한다.
13. will 다음에는 동사원형을 쓴다.
14. ① 현재진행형: be동사+동사원형-ing
② 미래시제: will+동사원형
③ 과거시제: 동사의 과거형 made
15. '주어+be going to+동사원형'의 순서로 쓴다.

UNIT 02 미래시제의 부정문과 의문문

A 1. 그들은 도서관에 갈 거예요.
→ 그들은 도서관에 가지 않을 거예요.
2. 나는 밖에서 놀 거예요.
→ 나는 밖에서 놀지 않을 거예요.
우리는 그 쇼를 볼 거예요.
→ 우리는 그 쇼를 보지 않을 거예요.

B 1. 그녀는 그 회의에 참석할 거예요.
→ 그녀는 그 회의에 참석할 건가요?
- 네, 그럴 거예요. / 아니요, 안 그럴 거예요.
2. 그들은 그 집을 팔 거예요.
→ 그들은 그 집을 팔 건가요?
- 네, 그럴 거예요. / 아니요, 안 그럴 거예요.

My Grammar Notes p.23

1. will, not, won't, Will 2. not, going to

Step1 Warm-Up p.24-25

A 1. will√join 2. will√go 3. will√pass
4. will√have 5. are√going to
6. am√going to 7. are√going to
8. is√going to

B 1. It won't[It'll not] 2. I'm not going to
3. She's not going to[She isn't going to]
4. I won't[I'll not]
5. They're not going to[They aren't going to]
6. Jack's not going to[Jack isn't going to]
7. He won't[He'll not] 8. Eric won't

C 1. Is 2. Will 3. Am 4. Are 5. Will
6. Is

D 1. he won't 2. they will 3. I am[we are]
4. she is 5. he isn't 6. I won't

Step2 Practice p.26-29

A 1. will not 2. rain 3. stay 4. isn't
5. work 6. invite 7. won't

B 1. Am, you are 2. Will she
3. No, he won't 4. Is, he is
5. Are, we aren't[I'm not]

C 1. won't call 2. won't[will not] meet
3. will study 4. won't[will not] win
5. will take 6. won't[will not] be
7. will have 8. won't[will not] speak

D 1. not going to visit
2. isn't[is not] going to stay
3. is going to get
4. aren't[are not] going to eat
5. is going to buy
6. aren't[are not] going to pay
7. aren't[are not] going to be
8. is going to take

E 1. Will the class start
2. Are you going to meet
3. Will they keep
4. Is the train going to leave
5. Is Rachel going to learn
6. Will you marry 7. Will you lend
8. Is he going to take
9. Are you going to give
10. Is the concert going to end

F 1. be 2. will not 3. sell
4. are not going to 5. are not going
6. Will 7. Is 8. Is the baby 9. going to
10. Will you buy 11. Will she make
12. they won't 13. they are 14. he will
15. we aren't 16. I will

Step3 Grammar into Writing p.30-31

A

A: Will it be sunny on Friday?
B: No, it won't. It will be snowy.
A: Will it be snowy on Saturday?
B: No, it won't. It will be rainy.
A: How about Sunday? I'm going to take a drive.
B: It will be sunny. But I'm sad.
A: What's wrong?
B: My class is going to go on a picnic on Monday. It's going to be cloudy.
A: Oh, that's too bad.

B 1. He isn't going to wash his car today.
2. Will you go to Kelly's birthday party?
3. Are you going to buy some chocolate?
4. I'm not going to answer the phone.
5. I will not[won't] have lunch with Brad.
6. Will you forgive him?

C
1. She will exercise every day.
2. She will read a lot of books.
3. She will study hard.
4. She will clean her room.
5. She won't tell lies.
6. She won't get up late.
7. She won't fight with her sister.

Wrap-Up Test

p.32-34

1. ⑤ **2.** ① **3.** ② **4.** ⑤ **5.** ④ **6.** ③
7. ④ **8.** ④ **9.** ② **10.** ③ **11.** ③
12. No, I'm not **13.** Yes, it will
14. The farmers are not going to grow vegetables next year.
15. Ted will not come early.

1. ①② 과거시제, ③ 현재시제, ④ 현재진행시제
2. Will+주어+동사원형 ~?
3. 주어+be going to+동사원형
4. will not = won't
5. ④ They are not going to stay in a hotel.
6. 미래에 대해 이야기하고 있으므로 will과 be going to를 이용한다.
7. ①②③⑤ Are[are], ④ will
8. be going to는 미래를 나타내므로 과거를 나타내는 부사 yesterday(어제)와 함께 쓸 수 없다.
9. ② won't는 will not의 줄임말이므로 뒤에 not을 쓸 수 없다.
10. 미래시제의 부정문: 주어+will not[won't]+동사원형 / 주어+be not going to+동사원형
11. 미래시제 질문에 대해 과거시제로 대답하는 것은 어색하다.
③ No, he wasn't. → No, he isn't.
12. 꽃을 살 것이라고 대답했으므로 빈칸에는 부정의 답이 와야 자연스럽다.
13. 밖에서 눈사람을 만들 것이라고 대답했으므로 빈칸에는 긍정의 답이 와야 자연스럽다.
14. 주어+be not going to+동사원형
15. will이 쓰인 문장의 부정문은 will 뒤에 not을 써서 나타낸다.

UNIT 03 시제 비교

B 아이들은 도넛을 매우 좋아해요.
그는 일요일마다 늦게 일어나요.
Joe는 지금 TV를 보고 있어요.

C 1. 나는 나의 친구들과 캠핑을 갈 거예요.
Susan은 그녀의 방을 청소할 예정이에요.
2. 그는 내일 한국을 떠날 거예요.
당신은 오늘 밤 피자를 먹을 건가요?

My Grammar Notes

p.37

1. played, will play 2. 현재진행형[현재진행시제]
3. going, 현재진행형[현재진행시제]

Step1 Warm-Up

p.38-39

A 1. ⓑ, ⓕ 2. ⓐ 3. ⓒ 4. ⓓ, ⓔ

B 1. is talking 2. gets up 3. is crying
4. go 5. reads

C 1. O 2. X 3. O 4. O 5. X 6. O 7. X 8. O

D 1. broke 2. takes 3. are shaking
4. will wear 5. played 6. is surfing
7. take 8. are going to ride

Step2 Practice

p.40-43

A 1. rained 2. runs 3. came
4. is reading 5. visited 6. will buy
7. traveled 8. are eating 9. go
10. waters

B 1. ⓑ 2. ⓒ 3. ⓓ 4. ⓐ

C 1. ② 2. ③ 3. ② 4. ④ 5. ① 6. ②

D 1. on Sundays 2. right now
3. next year 4. on Sundays
5. yesterday 6. next year

E 1. jumped 2. will[am going to] visit
3. ate 4. is reading 5. is practicing
6. takes 7. is

F 1. is traveling 2. won't[isn't going to]
3. didn't[did not] eat
4. are going[are going to go / will go]
5. is playing 6. left 7. have

G 1. Tim wrote e-mails
2. We aren't[are not] watching TV
3. Will you wear new jeans
4. Dad is cooking dinner for us
5. Jennifer helped her mother
6. This bakery is going to open
7. They sang and danced
8. My family is moving to Seoul
9. He is closing the window
10. Did she go scuba diving

Step3 Grammar into Writing

p.44-45

A 1. He lost his umbrella a few hours ago.
2. Are you doing your homework now?
3. John is not[isn't] going to sell the car.
4. We take an English test every Monday.
5. Did you watch the game last night?

B 1. 1) take 2) Daniel goes to the pool on weekends.
2. 1) are playing
2) Joe is talking on the phone now.
3. 1) Did, fix
2) Did she go hiking yesterday?
4. 1) going to wash
2) Katie is going to get a haircut tomorrow.

C 1. celebrates 2. am wearing
3. visited 4. will[are going to] make

Wrap-Up Test

p.46-48

1. ② **2.** ⑤ **3.** is **4.** ④ **5.** ② **6.** ③
7. ⑤ **8.** ② **9.** ③ **10.** ③ **11.** ①
12. Was, will go **13.** celebrate, had
14. Did you finish your work
15. We are having chicken on Friday.
[On Friday, we are having chicken.]

1. yesterday가 쓰였으므로 과거시제가 되어야 한다.
2. ⑤ an hour ago는 과거시제와 함께 쓴다.
3. 현재진행시제: be동사+동사원형-ing,
미래시제의 부정문: be not going to+동사원형
4. ①②③⑤ 미래, ④ 현재진행
5. last Saturday는 과거시제와, next weekend는 미래시제와 함께 쓰는 것이 자연스럽다. 시간을

나타내는 미래 부사구와 함께 쓰이면 현재진행형으로도 가까운 미래의 일을 나타낼 수 있다.

6. ①②④⑤ 과거, ③ 현재진행

7. right now는 현재진행과, soon은 미래시제와 함께 쓰는 것이 자연스럽다.

8. 첫 번째 문장은 every morning과 함께 쓰여 반복되는 습관을 나타내므로 현재시제를, last Tuesday는 지난 일을 나타내므로 과거시제를 쓰는 것이 자연스럽다.

9. ③ cried → is crying

10. ③ 어젯밤에 뉴스를 보았냐는 질문에 긍정의 대답을 하고 나서, 지금 보고 있다고 말하는 것은 어색하다.

11. ① goes → went

12. A에는 last year를 써서 과거를 나타내므로 과거시제를, B에는 next year과 함께 미래시제를 쓰는 것이 자연스럽다.

13. A에는 every year를 써서 현재의 지속적 사실을 나타내므로 현재시제를, B에는 last Christmas와 함께 과거시제를 쓰는 것이 자연스럽다.

14. 일반동사의 과거시제 의문문: Did+주어+동사원형 ~?

15. 현재진행시제로 가까운 미래를 나타내기도 한다.

UNIT 04 can, must, may

A Jessica는 그곳에 갈 수 있어요.
당신은 그곳에 가야 해요.

B 1. 나는 수영을 할 수 있어요.
우리는 그 일을 끝낼 수 있어요.
Alex는 요리를 잘할 수 있어요.

2. 당신은 창문을 열어도 좋아요.
당신은 창문을 열 수 있어요.

C 나는 그를 기다려야 해요.
당신은 수업 시간에 조용히 해야 해요.
Monica는 그 책을 읽어야 해요.

D 들어가도 될까요?
당신은 내 전화기를 사용해도 돼요.

My Grammar Notes p.51

1. 동사원형 2. able 3. must 4. may

Step1 Warm-Up p.52-53

A 1. must 2. can 3. may 4. will
5. must 6. can 7. will 8. may

B 1. 1) go 2) goes 2. 1) save 2) buy
3. 1) speaks 2) speak
4. 1) finished 2) play
5. 1) likes 2) make

C 1. ~해야 한다 2. ~할 수 있다 3. ~해도 좋다
4. ~해야 한다 5. ~해야 한다 6. ~할 수 있다
7. ~해도 좋다 8. ~할 수 있다

D 1. am able to 2. has to 3. is able to
4. have to 5. may

Step2 Practice p.54-57

A 1. ⓐ 2. ⓑ 3. ⓐ 4. ⓒ 5. ⓒ 6. ⓑ
7. ⓑ 8. ⓐ 9. ⓐ 10. ⓑ 11. ⓑ 12. ⓒ
13. ⓒ 14. ⓒ 15. ⓐ

B 1. is able to 2. has to 3. can
4. must 5. are able to 6. may

C 1. am able to 2. is able to 3. visit
4. must[have to] 5. has to
6. can count 7. must follow

D 1. O 2. X 3. O 4. O 5. X

E 1. ② 2. ② 3. ② 4. ①

F 1. can write 2. must stay
3. may wear[can wear] 4. can speak

5. must practice 6. can finish
7. may have[can have] 8. can contact
9. must go 10. can change

Step3 Grammar into Writing

p.58-59

A
1. You must clean your room.
2. Joe is able to make pasta.
3. He has to fix the door.
4. She can drive a truck.
5. You can leave now.
6. They must start the show before 7.

B
1. Cindy is able to bake cakes.
2. He has to get up early tomorrow.
3. I'm able to write stories in English.
4. She is able to skate very well.
5. You have to wait in line.
6. I have to buy a gift for my sister.
7. We are able to make films with smartphones.

C

This is Future Town. There are many robots here. The robots look like humans. They can be able to think and act like humans. They must helps people in danger. Some robots can even flying and saving people. These robots are really cool!

↓

This is Future Town. There are many robots here. The robots look like humans. They can[are able to] think and act like humans. They must help people in danger. Some robots can even fly and save people. These robots are really cool!

Wrap-Up Test

p.60-62

1. ② **2.** ① **3.** ⑤ **4.** ② **5.** ④ **6.** ①
7. ③ **8.** ⑤ **9.** ② **10.** ④ **11.** ①
12. have to **13.** are able to ride
14. may buy this bag
15. have to → has to

1. be able to는 조동사 can으로 바꾸어 쓸 수 있다.
2. 의미상 '~해야 한다'가 되어야 하므로 must나 have to가 적절하다.
3. ⑤ may: ~해도 좋다
4. '~할 수 있다'를 뜻하는 can을 이용한다.
5. '~해야 한다'를 뜻하는 must를 이용한다.
6. 조동사 뒤에는 항상 동사원형을 쓴다.
7. ③ ~할 수 있다, ①②④⑤ ~해도 좋다(= may)
8. ⑤ be able to는 '~할 수 있다'라는 뜻으로, 상대방의 능력을 나타내는 말은 빈칸에 적절하지 않다.
9. ② ~할 수 있다, ①③④⑤ ~해도 좋다(= may)
10. 조동사 뒤에는 동사원형이 온다.
④ solved → solve
11. ② is able to sing → are able to sing
③ may wants → may want
④ has to is → has to be
⑤ may ordering → may order
12. 의미상 '~해야 한다'라는 뜻의 have to가 적절하다.
13. be able to + 동사원형: ~할 수 있다
14. '~해도 좋다'라는 허가의 의미를 나타낼 때는 조동사 may 혹은 can을 이용하며, 뒤에 동사원형을 쓴다.
15. 주어가 3인칭 단수일 때는 have to 대신 has to를 쓴다.

UNIT 05 조동사의 부정문

B 1. 그는 수영을 잘하지 못해요.
우리는 테니스를 못 쳐요.
2. 당신은 오늘 밤 밖에 나가면 안 돼요.
그 상자는 그녀의 것이에요.
당신은 그것을 열어서는 안 돼요.
당신은 그것을 열 수 없어요.

C 1. 당신은 밖에서 놀아서는 안 돼요.
우리는 거짓말을 하면 안 돼요.
2. 당신은 점심 도시락을 가져올 필요가 없어요.
그는 나에게 전화할 필요가 없어요.

D 당신은 이곳에 주차하면 안 돼요.

My Grammar Notes p.65

1. not, 동사원형, cannot[can't], not
2. may 3. have to

Step1 Warm-Up p.66-67

A 1. ② 2. ② 3. ① 4. ② 5. ②

B 1. can't finish 2. aren't able to
3. must not eat 4. doesn't have to
5. may not go 6. can't wear

C 1. can't 2. must not[mustn't]
3. don't have to 4. may not
5. doesn't have to
6. is not[isn't] able to

D 1. can't 2. may not 3. don't have to
4. must 5. can 6. must not

Step2 Practice p.68-71

A 1. am not able to 2. is not[isn't] able to
3. X 4. X 5. are not[aren't] able to
6. am not able to 7. is not[isn't] able to

B 1. must not 2. don't have to
3. don't have to 4. mustn't 5. must not
6. doesn't have to 7. mustn't

C 1. O 2. O 3. O 4. X 5. X 6. O

D 1. doesn't have to 2. must not
3. dance 4. may not bring
5. aren't able to 6. can't go

E 1. can't 2. can't 3. is 4. can't 5. may
6. may 7. must 8. may not 9. have to
10. must 11. can 12. have to 13. isn't
14. mustn't 15. doesn't have to

F 1. must not swim 2. must keep
3. cannot[can't] find
4. mustn't[cannot/can't] tell
5. don't have to go 6. is able to
7. doesn't have to attend
8. are not able to 9. has to have

Step3 Grammar into Writing p.72-73

A 1. She must not travel alone.
2. We don't have to go to school tomorrow.
3. I cannot[can't] drive a car.
4. You may not smoke in this building.
5. She doesn't have to come early.
6. We aren't[are not] able to solve the riddle.

B 1. I cannot[can't] find my watch.
2. You must not[mustn't] pick the flowers.
3. He doesn't have to work today.
4. You cannot[may not] bring your dog

inside.

5. You don't have to meet Alice today.

6. The baby birds are not[aren't] able to fly.

C 1. must know

2. may not[mustn't/must not/cannot] wear

3. have to[must]

4. must not[mustn't/may not/cannot]

Wrap-Up Test

p.74-76

1. ② **2.** ④ **3.** ⑤ **4.** ① **5.** ③ **6.** ⑤

7. ② **8.** ③ **9.** ⑤ **10.** ④

11. is not able to **12.** must[may] not

13. may not → doesn't have to

14. You cannot bring drinks.

15. (1) have to (2) can't (3) aren't

1. 상자가 너무 무겁다고 했으므로 (상자를) 들 수 없다는 말이 적절하다.

2. 어조상 강한 금지를 나타내는 must not이 적절하다.

3. 너무 위험하다고 했으므로, 빈칸에는 금지를 나타내는 표현이 와야 한다.
①②③④ ~해서는 안 된다, ⑤ ~할 필요가 없다

4. '~할 수 없다'의 be not able to는 cannot으로 바꾸어 쓸 수 있다.

5. 열쇠가 없어서 문을 열 수 없으므로 첫 번째 빈칸에는 cannot이, 공원에 쓰레기를 버리면 안 되므로 두 번째 빈칸에는 금지를 나타내는 must[may not]이 적절하다.

6. don't[doesn't] have to: ~할 필요가 없다

7. ① → are not able to sit
③ → cannot wash
④ → doesn't have to borrow
⑤ → may not walk

8. ③ have to의 부정은 don't[doesn't] have to이다.

9. ⑤ be not able to는 '~할 수 없다'라는 뜻으로, 불가능을 나타낸다.

10. ④ must use not → must not use

11. 불가능의 의미를 갖는 cannot이므로 be not able to와 바꿔 쓸 수 있다.

12. 도서관에서 조용히 해야 한다는 내용 뒤에 소음을 낸다는 make noise가 이어지고 있으므로, 이를 금지하는 must[may] not이 들어가야 한다.

13. don't[doesn't] have to: ~할 필요가 없다

14. cannot+동사원형: ~해서는 안 된다

15. (1) 어른은 10달러, 어린이는 5달러의 입장료를 내야 한다.
(2) 월요일은 휴무이다.
(3) 박물관은 오전 9시부터 오후 5시까지 문을 연다.

UNIT 06 조동사의 의문문

B 그녀는 스노보드를 탈 수 있나요?
- 네, 탈 수 있어요. / 아니요, 타지 못해요.
저를 위해 노래를 불러 주실래요?
- 물론이죠. / 죄송하지만, 안 돼요.
나가서 놀아도 될까요?
- 그럼요. / 아니요, 안 돼요.

C Billy는 시험을 쳐야 하나요?
- 네, 그래야 해요. / 아니요, 그럴 필요 없어요.

My Grammar Notes

p.79

1. 조동사, 주어 2. Are, able to

3. Can 4. May, use 5. I have to

Step1 Warm-Up p.80-81

A 1. Can you 2. Must I 3. May I
4. Is she 5. Do I 6. Can you

B 1. follow 2. speak 3. I use 4. able to
5. I learn 6. Can I 7. Do I have to
8. Is your dad able to

C 1. Must 2. Could 3. May 4. Must
5. Can 6. Must

D 1. ⓓ 2. ⓐ 3. ⓕ 4. ⓒ 5. ⓑ 6. ⓔ

Step2 Practice p.82-85

A 1. Can, May 2. Can 3. Can, May
4. Can 5. Must 6. Must 7. Can

B 1. X 2. O 3. X 4. O

C 1. Can, sing 2. Must, tell
3. Can, rest 4. Can, answer
5. May, wear 6. May, park
7. Must, pay

D 1. I can 2. he can't 3. you must
4. you may 5. they can't
6. I don't have to[we don't have to]
7. you can't 8. you may not

E 1. Can you run, ⓕ 2. Can I use, ⓖ
3. Must they clean, ⓗ 4. May I ask, ⓓ
5. Are you able to ride, ⓔ
6. Does Ethan have to attend, ⓒ
7. Can they stay, ⓐ
8. Must I hand in, ⓑ

F 1. Are you able to see
2. Must I wear[Do I have to wear]
3. Can you go 4. Can[May] I go
5. Can she play[Is she able to play]
6. Does Sophia have to[Must Sophia]

G 1. Could you cook 2. May I turn on
3. Can she join 4. Must I take
5. Is Lisa able to 6. Do we have to

Step3 Grammar into Writing p.86-87

A 1. Can I help you?
2. Can I get up late tomorrow?
3. May I turn on the music?
4. Do I have to eat those vegetables?
5. Are you able to understand the book?

B 1. 1) May I 2) May I use your pen?
2. 1) Can you 2) Can you drive?
3. 1) Must we
2) Must I wear sneakers at the gym?
4. 1) Can[Will/Could/Would] you
2) Can[Will/Could/Would] you open the door?
5. 1) Do, have to
2) Do we have to wait here?

C 1. May I use 2. No, you may not.
3. must not talk 4. Yes, you can.

Wrap-Up Test p.88-90

1. ③ **2.** ⑤ **3.** ② **4.** Are bears able to
5. ③ **6.** ⑤ **7.** ④ **8.** ① **9.** ① **10.** ④
11. ③ **12.** ③ **13.** must[may] not be
14. Do I have to wear a seat belt?
15. May[Can] I, mustn't[cannot/can't]

1. May[Can] I ~?: 제가 ~해도 될까요? (허락, 허가)

2. Must you do ~? = Do you have to ~?
당신은 ~해야 하나요? (의무)

3. 첫 번째 빈칸에는 요청의 의미로 쓰인 can, 두 번째 빈칸에는 능력의 의미로 쓰인 can이 오는 것이 알맞다.

4. 능력을 나타내는 can은 be able to로 바꿔 쓸 수 있다.

5. Must I ~?: ~해야 하나요? (의무)
May[Can] I ~?: ~해도 될까요? (허락, 허가)

6. ①②③④ ~해도 좋다 (허락), ⑤ ~할 수 있다 (능력)

7. '~할 필요가 없다'라는 뜻의 don't have to로 답하고 있으므로, 빈칸에는 의무의 조동사 must를 이용한 의문문이 와야 한다.

8. ① May → Must

9. 의무를 나타내는 조동사의 의문문:
Does she have to + 동사원형~?
= Must she + 동사원형~?: 그녀가 ~해야 하나요?

10. ④ B가 거절해야 하는 상황이므로 you can't가 아닌 I can't가 적절하다.

11. 조동사 다음에는 동사원형을 쓴다.
③ plays → play

12. A의 요청을 거절해야 하는 상황이므로 you can이 아닌 you can't가 적절하다.

13. must[may] not + 동사원형: ~해서는 안 된다

14. Do I have to ~?: 제가 ~해야 하나요?

15. May[Can] I ~?: 제가 ~해도 될까요? (허가, 허락)
must not[mustn't/can't/cannot]: ~해서는 안 된다 (금지)

UNIT 07 부사

C 1. 나는 일찍 일어나요.
그는 열심히 공부해요.
2. 우리는 정말 좋은 친구들이에요.
이 만화책은 무척 흥미로워요.
3. 그는 매우 빨리 달릴 수 있어요.
나의 언니는 수영을 매우 잘해요.
4. 슬프게도, 우리는 야구 경기에서 졌어요.
갑자기, 비가 그쳤어요.

My Grammar Notes p.93

1. 부사 2. sadly, happily, 형용사, well
3. 동사, 형용사, 부사

Step1 Warm-Up p.94-95

A 1. ① 2. ③ 3. ② 4. ① 5. ③ 6. ①
7. ④ 8. ②

B 1. easily 2. high 3. tonight 4. hard
5. outside 6. really 7. Luckily 8. fast

C 1. sadly, ⓒ 2. beautifully, ⓐ
3. lightly, ⓑ 4. quietly, ⓗ
5. easily, ⓔ 6. carefully, ⓖ
7. fast, ⓕ 8. well, ⓓ 9. nicely, ⓘ

D 1. read 2. beautiful 3. hard
4. gets up 5. I don't like him
6. smiles 7. lazy 8. much

Step2 Practice p.96-99

A 1. quickly 2. early 3. cheerfully
4. busily 5. fast 6. luckily 7. well
8. sadly 9. recently 10. loudly
11. safely 12. softly 13. simply
14. fortunately 15. gently
16. peacefully

B 1. slowly 2. happily 3. high
4. quickly 5. hard 6. kindly

C 1. really 2. happy 3. late 4. nice
5. quickly 6. good 7. Suddenly
8. easily

D 1. hard 2. fast 3. beautifully 4. well
5. carefully 6. happily

E 1. really 2. loudly 3. easily 4. well
5. late 6. Luckily 7. suddenly
8. quietly 9. quickly 10. Sadly

F 1. high 2. wisely 3. arrived early
4. recently 5. hard 6. perfectly
7. Honestly 8. fast

G 1. good → well 2. Sudden → Suddenly
3. well → good 4. Final → Finally
5. politely → polite 6. lately → late
7. clear very → very clear
8. greatly → great

Step3 Grammar into Writing p.100-101

A 1. ⓔ, He always drives gently.
2. ⓒ, Kids grow up quickly.
3. ⓑ, Fortunately, he got a free ticket.
4. ⓓ, She arrived at the hotel early.
5. ⓐ, I am very busy today.
6. ⓕ, You must listen to me carefully.

B 1. She studied math hard.
2. He is waiting for you outside.
3. Eric rides a horse very well.
4. Sally answered the question kindly.
5. I opened the door quietly.

C

I'm a baby kangaroo. I live in a pocket on my mom's stomach. The pocket is very largely and cozy. My mom always carries me in her pocket safe. She can hop really highly. So, lucky, I can go everywhere with her.

1. largely → large 2. safe → safely
3. highly → high 4. lucky → luckily

Wrap-Up Test p.102-104

1. ④ **2.** ② **3.** ① **4.** ③ **5.** ②, ④, ⑤
6. loudly **7.** ① **8.** ⑤ **9.** ③ **10.** ①
11. ④ **12.** ④ **13.** very slowly
14. You speak Korean well.
15. Fortunately, she caught the last train.

1. ④ 동사(do)를 수식하는 부사가 와야 한다. good은 형용사이다.
2. ①③④⑤ 형용사-부사, ② 명사-형용사
3. 동사(practice)와 명사(work)를 모두 수식해야 하므로 부사와 형용사의 형태가 같은 hard가 적절하다.
4. be동사와 일반동사(study)를 모두 보충 설명해야 하므로 형용사와 부사의 형태가 같은 late가 적절하다.
5. ②④⑤ 부사 ①③ 형용사
6. quietly(조용히) ↔ loudly(큰 소리로)
7. 첫 번째 빈칸에는 동사(work)를 수식하는 부사가, 두 번째 빈칸에는 명사(delivery)를 수식하는 형용사가 와야 한다. 첫 번째 빈칸에는 의미상 late가 자연스럽다. (lately: 최근에)
8. 첫 번째 빈칸에는 문장 전체를 수식하는 부사가, 두 번째 빈칸 앞에는 감각동사(feels)가 쓰였으므로 형용사가, 세 번째 빈칸에는 부사(fast)를 수식하는 부사가 와야 한다.
9. 보기의 부사는 형용사(interesting)를 수식한다.
① 문장 전체 수식 ② 동사구(get up) 수식
③ 형용사(moving) 수식 ④ 부사(fast) 수식
⑤ 부사(late) 수식
10. ① '높이'라는 뜻일 때는 부사 high를 쓴다. (highly: 매우)
11. ① honestly → honest ② greatly → great
③ lowly → low ⑤ friendly는 형용사
12. ④ easy → easily
13. '아주 느린 택시 운전사'라는 의미이므로 형용사 slow를 부사로 바꿔서 very와 함께 문장을 완성

한다.

14. 동사(speak)를 꾸미는 부사 well을 쓴다.

15. 주어진 문장은 '다행히도 마지막 기차를 잡아 탔다' 라는 뜻이다. 따라서 문장 전체를 수식하는 형용사 Fortunate은 부사 Fortunately로, 명사(train)를 수식하는 부사(lastly)는 형용사 last로 바꿔 쓴다.

UNIT 08 빈도부사

B 1. 그는 항상 친절하고 신사적이다.
L.A.는 보통 날씨가 맑다.
나는 피아노 수업에 종종 늦는다.
너는 가끔 내 책들을 빌릴 수 있다.
우리는 이 건물에서 담배를 피우면 절대 안 된다.
2. 나는 저녁 식사 후에 항상 산책한다.
Patrick은 대개 카페에서 커피를 마신다.
그들은 여름에 종종 야영하러 간다.
Brown 씨는 때때로 불쌍한 사람들을 돕는다.
우리는 일요일에 절대 공부하지 않는다.

C 당신은 얼마나 자주 학교에 늦나요?
- 저는 학교에 절대 늦지 않아요.
그녀는 얼마나 자주 운동하나요?
- 그녀는 가끔 운동해요.
- 그녀는 일요일마다 체육관에 가요.

My Grammar Notes p.107

1. usually, sometimes, never
2. 조동사, 일반동사 3. how often, How often

Step1 Warm-Up p.108-109

A 1. never 2. usually 3. sometimes
4. often 5. always 6. often

B 1. always 2. often 3. sometimes
4. never 5. usually 6. sometimes

C 1. ② 2. ① 3. ① 4. ① 5. ① 6. ①
7. ① 8. ①

D 1. ⓒ 2. ⓐ 3. ⓔ 4. ⓑ 5. ⓓ

Step2 Practice p.110-113

A 1. must always 2. often takes
3. never gets 4. always goes
5. can sometimes 6. never arrives
7. usually spend

B 1. ③ → ② → ① 2. ③ → ② → ①
3. ① → ③ → ② 4. ③ → ① → ②

C 1. F 2. T 3. T 4. T 5. F

D 1. usually gets 2. will never be
3. How often do you
4. must always tell
5. sometimes forgets
6. Do Americans usually eat

E 1. ⓑ 2. ⓐ 3. ⓓ 4. ⓒ

F 1. They eat junk food three times a week.
2. You can always download music.
3. She never goes to dance parties.
4. I climb mountains once a year.
5. It rains almost every day in London.

G 1. will always remember
2. never listens 3. sometimes goes
4. is always 5. will never say
6. always rises 7. can always come
8. usually have 9. How often do you go
10. How often does Paul swim

11. sometimes covers

12. What do you usually do

Step3 Grammar into Writing p.114-115

A
1. must always be careful on roads
2. sometimes freezes in winter
3. Daniel sometimes falls asleep in class.
4. I always take a nap after lunch.
5. Brian usually goes to bed at 10.
6. I often buy a gift for my little brother.
7. She never sees horror movies.
8. They are always busy in the morning.

B
1. He usually goes to the library
2. Alice will never be late for
3. How often do you go
4. I can always send e-mails
5. She sometimes takes a walk

C

Sean always is busy every morning. He must get on the school bus. The school bus usually arrive at 8 a.m. But it sometimes is 10 minutes late. How often do he miss the bus? Never! On the bus, he sits often next to his best friend Rolla.

↓

Sean is always busy every morning. He must get on the school bus. The school bus usually arrives at 8 a.m. But it is sometimes 10 minutes late. How often does he miss the bus? Never! On the bus, he often sits next to his best friend Rolla.

Wrap-Up Test p.116-118

1. ① **2.** ② **3.** ③ **4.** ⑤ **5.** ③
6. ③-①-② **7.** ① **8.** ⑤ **9.** ② **10.** ④
11. ⑤ **12.** He usually gets good grades in math. **13.** How often can she play games? **14.** must always brush your teeth **15.** can give sometimes → can sometimes give

1. 빈도부사는 보통 일반동사(watches) 앞에 쓴다.

2. 빈도부사는 조동사(can) 뒤, 일반동사(take) 앞에 쓴다.

3. ③ You must help✓ → You must✓help

4. 빈도부사는 보통 일반동사 앞에 위치하며, 주어가 3인칭 단수이므로 동사에 -s를 붙인다.

5. ③ how often 의문문에는 Yes나 No로 대답하지 않는다.

6. always (항상) → usually (보통) → sometimes (때때로)

7. 빈도부사는 보통 조동사(will) 뒤, 일반동사(drink) 앞에 오며, 빈도부사 never는 그 자체로 부정의 의미가 있으므로 not과 함께 쓰지 않는다.

8. 여기서 do가 일반동사이고 Alex가 3인칭 단수이므로 never does가 적절하고, 빈도부사 always는 일반동사(listen) 앞에 쓴다.

9. ② sometimes는 '때때로'의 의미이다.

10. never는 not과 함께 쓰지 않는다.
④ isn't never → is never 또는 isn't

11. ⑤ how often으로 물었으므로 빈도나 횟수를 나타내는 말로 대답해야 한다.

12. 빈도부사는 보통 일반동사(get) 앞에 쓴다.

13. '얼마나 자주 ~?'를 물을 때는 'How often+조동사+주어+동사원형 ~?'의 어순을 따른다.

14. '~해야 한다'라고 했으므로 의무의 조동사 must를 쓰며, always(항상)는 빈도부사는 보통 조동사 뒤, 일반동사(brush) 앞에 쓴다.

15. 빈도부사는 보통 조동사(can) 뒤, 일반동사(give) 앞에 쓴다.

UNIT 09 숫자 표현

My Grammar Notes

p.121

2. thirds **3.** nineteen **4.** 요일, 연도

Step1 Warm-Up

p.122-123

A **1.** three, third **2.** five, fifth
3. eight, eighth **4.** nine, ninth
5. twelve, twelfth
6. eighteen, eighteenth
7. twenty-two, twenty-second
8. thirty, thirtieth **9.** fifty-one, fifty-first
10. forty-three, forty-third

B **1.** a half **2.** one third **3.** two thirds
4. one fourth **5.** three fifths
6. three fourths **7.** five sixths
8. three sevenths **9.** five ninths
10. nine elevenths

C **1.** ⓔ **2.** ⓑ **3.** ⓓ **4.** ⓐ **5.** ⓒ **6.** ⓗ **7.** ⓕ
8. ⓖ

D **1.** August 15 **2.** December 10
3. February 5, 1920 **4.** June 18, 2010
5. October 9, 2017 **6.** Monday, March 1
7. Friday, April 9 **8.** Tuesday, July 24

Step2 Practice

p.124-127

A **1.** two **2.** the third **3.** the fourth
4. the fifth **5.** the third
6. thirteenth **7.** fifteen **8.** first
9. twenty-first
10. one hundred and fifty

B **1.** three fourths **2.** $\frac{1}{5}$
3. two thirds **4.** $\frac{1}{2}$
5. three fifths **6.** $\frac{5}{9}$
7. a[one] third **8.** $\frac{4}{7}$
9. a[one] sixth **10.** $\frac{1}{4}$

C **1.** nineteen ninety-nine
2. twenty fifty-five /
two thousand (and) fifty-five
3. twenty thirty-four /
two thousand (and) thirty-four
4. seventeen fifty-six
5. two thousand (and) two /
twenty oh two
6. two thousand
7. sixteen sixty
8. twenty twelve /
two thousand (and) twelve
9. eighteen ninety-five
10. nineteen forty-four
11. two thousand (and) nine /
twenty oh nine
12. nineteen oh one
13. fourteen hundred
14. eighteen eighty-eight

D **1.** April 5 **2.** May 22(nd)
3. December 25(th), 2010
4. November 13(th), 1999
5. September 4(th), 2018
6. January 17(th), 2002
7. Saturday, August 10(th)
8. Friday, March 3(rd)

9. Sunday, July 8(th), 2020
10. Monday, June 7(th), 2021

E 1. ② 2. ② 3. ① 4. ③ 5. ③ 6. ①
7. ③ 8. ③ 9. ③ 10. ② 11. ②

F 1. five 2. the first 3. the third
4. the fifth 5. eight 6. eleven
7. the seventh 8. the second 9. twelve

G 1. the second 2. three
3. three fourths[three quarters]
4. seven 5. April 30(th), 2021
6. June 6(th) 7. first

Step3 Grammar into Writing p.128-129

A 1. My brother is twelve years old.
2. Jeff lost three fifths of the money.
3. This is my second audition.
4. Minho is one hundred and eighty centimeters tall.
5. Today is Wednesday, March 7(th), 2019.

B 1. the one hundredth
2. Monday, July 9(th) 3. nine
4. the fourth 5. a[one] third
6. forty-five 7. May 8(th) 8. sixtieth

C 1. twenty-third
2. Saturday, February 20(th), 2020
3. three fifths
4. eleventh floor

Wrap-Up Test p.130-132

1. ③ **2.** ④ **3.** ⑤ **4.** ① **5.** ⑤ **6.** ②
7. ④ **8.** ② **9.** ③ **10.** the second
11. a[one] half **12.** ③
13. We have a[one] thousand guests.
He is our hundredth[one hundredth] guest.
14. (1) first (2) An eleventh (3) two
15. seven days

1. ③ twelve – twelfth

2. ① a[one] third ② two thirds ③ three fourths ⑤ a[one] ninths

3. ① twelve hundred ② sixteen fifty
③ two thousand (and) three
④ two thousand (and) nine

4-5. 순서(~ 번째)를 나타낼 때는 서수, 개수를 나타낼 때는 기수를 쓴다.

6. ② ten → the tenth

7. ④ thirthieth → thirty

8. '요일–월–일–연도'의 순으로 쓴다.

9. 분자가 1일 때는 분모에 -s를 붙이지 않는다.
③ a thirds → a third

10. 둘째는 순서를 나타내는 말이므로 서수를 쓴다. 서수 앞에는 the를 쓴다.

11. 2분의 1(절반): a[one] half

12. 소요 시간을 표현할 때는 기수를 쓴다.
③ the second hours → two hours

13. 고객의 수가 천 명이므로 thousandth는 기수 a[one] thousand로, 그는 백 번째 손님이므로 hundred를 서수 (one) hundredth로 고쳐야 한다.

14. (1) 1월 21일은 영어 캠프 첫 번째 날이므로, first를 쓴다.
(2) 선생님 수는 참가자 수의 1/11이므로, an eleventh를 쓴다.

(3) 영어 캠프는 학생회관의 2개 층을 사용할 예정이므로, two가 와야 한다.

15. 영어 캠프는 7일간 열리므로, 기수 seven을 이용해 표현한다.

UNIT 10 문장의 형태

A 그 강아지는 귀여워 보여요.
그 감자 피자는 좋은 냄새가 나요.
레몬은 신맛이 나요.
그녀는 아주 피곤해해요.

B 내 친구들은 나를 좋아해요.
그녀는 자명종 시계를 가지고 있어요.
그는 새 자전거를 원해요.
우리는 우리의 계획을 바꿨어요.
나는 매일 아침 팬케이크를 먹어요.
나는 당신을 믿지 않아요.

C 나의 남자친구는 나에게 선물을 줬어요.
그는 우리에게 그의 앨범을 보여줬어요.
나의 언니는 나에게 그녀의 비밀들을 말해줬어요.
Ally의 아버지는 그녀에게 새 신발을 사주셨어요.
David는 당신에게 생일 케이크를 만들어 줄 거예요.
당신이 그들에게 돈을 좀 빌려줄래요?
이메일로 제게 보고서를 보내줄래요?
내 아버지는 우리에게 미국 역사를 가르치셨어요.

My Grammar Notes p.135

1. 형용사 **2.** 명사 **3.** ~에게

Step1 Warm-Up p.136-137

A 1. We feel good. → 주어+동사+형용사
2. He has a car. → 주어+동사+명사
3. She likes pizza. → 주어+동사+명사
4. It sounds fun. → 주어+동사+형용사
5. I gave him chocolate.
→ 주어+동사+대명사+명사
6. I bought Jenny a ring.
→ 주어+동사+명사+명사
7. The soup tastes bad. → 주어+동사+형용사
8. They took a taxi. → 주어+동사+명사

B 1. ⓓ 2. ⓑ 3. ⓗ 4. ⓔ 5. ⓒ 6. ⓕ 7. ⓐ 8. ⓖ

C 1. ① 2. ① 3. ① 4. ② 5. ①

D 1. her an e-mail 2. him a secret
3. his mother a scarf
4. my brother a sweater
5. me a science book
6. her his pictures 7. me English
8. his cousin a birthday card

Step2 Practice p.138-141

A 1. looks 2. smells 3. feel 4. sounds
5. smell 6. look 7. sounds 8. look

B 1. ③ 2. ② 3. ③ 4. ② 5. ③ 6. ① 7. ③

C 1. I study math
2. Jane reads a mystery novel
3. We brush our teeth
4. They ate lunch
5. She didn't take the bus
6. Mina will visit us
7. Lucas plays basketball
8. He will watch documentary
9. Many people remember the war.

D 1. me 2. him 3. her 4. you 5. them
6. us 7. my sister 8. his students

E 1. ② 2. ③ 3. ② 4. ② 5. ③ 6. ② 7. ①
8. ③

F 1. looks peaceful 2. feel sleepy
3. ate cereal 4. wants a new watch
5. told me the secret
6. sounds funny
7. bought me a hamburger
8. made my mom

G 1. This coffee smells great.
2. The actor's voice sounds wonderful.
3. I practice the guitar every day.
4. Ms. Lee teaches foreigners Korean.
5. Jennifer showed me her diary.

Step3 Grammar into Writing p.142-143

A 1. I feel bored. 2. She looks healthy.
3. She didn't change her mind.
4. I have a good idea.
5. He lent me his shoes.
6. We gave her a concert ticket.

B 1. 1) speaks
2) My uncle speaks German well.
2. 1) sent him
2) He sent me text messages.
3. 1) bought
2) My mom bought me a new bicycle.
4. 1) made
2) He made us a big snowman.

C 1. feels soft
2. invented this
3. showed people cotton candy
[showed cotton candy to people]
4. made them millions of dollars
[made millions of dollars for them]

Wrap-Up Test p.144-146

1. ③ **2.** ④ **3.** ③ **4.** ③ **5.** ⑤ **6.** ④
7. ④ **8.** ③ **9.** ③ **10.** ④ **11.** ④
12. looks
13. Will she tell her friends the story?
/ Will she tell the story to her friends?
14. gave the children a lot of presents
15. The boy writes a letter every day.

1. 동사 send는 '보내주다'의 의미로 쓰일 때 뒤에 명사 2개를 취하는데, 첫 번째 명사는 주로 '~에게'를 뜻하는 사람이다.

2. '~에게'에 해당하는 대명사는 목적격으로 쓴다.

3. '동사+명사'와 '동사+(대)명사+명사' 형태를 모두 취할 수 있는 동사는 buy이다.

4. ③ has 뒤에는 명사가 와야 한다.

5. ⑤ 감각동사 tasted 뒤에는 형용사가 와야 한다.

6. tell+명사(사람)+명사(사물): ~에게 …을 말해주다

7. 첫 번째 빈칸 뒤에 형용사(tired)가 이어지므로 감각동사(feel)를, 두 번째 빈칸 뒤에 명사(curry) 하나만 이어지므로 동사 ate를, 세 번째 빈칸 뒤에 대명사와 명사가 이어지므로 동사 bought를 쓰는 것이 적절하다. 두 번째 빈칸의 this morning은 명사가 아닌 부사구이다.

8. ①②④⑤ 동사+(대)명사+명사, ③ 동사+명사

9. ① salt → salty
② '~을'에 해당하는 명사 자리에 대명사를 쓸 수 없다. (gave me it → gave it to me)
④ happily → happy
⑤ the picture her → her the picture 또는 the picture to her

10. ④ made sandwhiches us → made us sandwiches 또는 made sandwhiches for us

11. ④ 네 옷에서 안 좋은 냄새가 나.

12. '동사(look)+형용사'의 형태이다.

13. '동사(tell)+명사(~에게)+명사(~을)'의 형태이다.

14. '동사(give)+명사(~에게)+명사(~을)'의 형태이다.

15. '동사(write)+명사(~을)'의 형태이다.

MEMO

MEMO

MEMO

MEMO

43 SINCE 1980 rd
Let's grow together
NE능률이
미래를
창조합니다.
건강한 배움의 고객가치를 제공하겠다는 꿈을 실현하기 위해
40년이 넘는 시간 동안 열심히 달려왔습니다.
앞으로도 끊임없는 연구와 노력을 통해
당연한 것을 멈추지 않고
고객, 기업, 직원 모두가 함께 성장하는 NE능률이 되겠습니다.
NE 능률

Beginning

Easy

Active

New

이제 시작이에요!
처음으로 문법을 공부하는 여러분, 두려워하지 마세요.
이제부터 Grammar Bean(그래머빈)이 영어에 대한
자신감을 가질 수 있게 도와줄게요.

구성과 특징

알기 쉬운 문법 설명

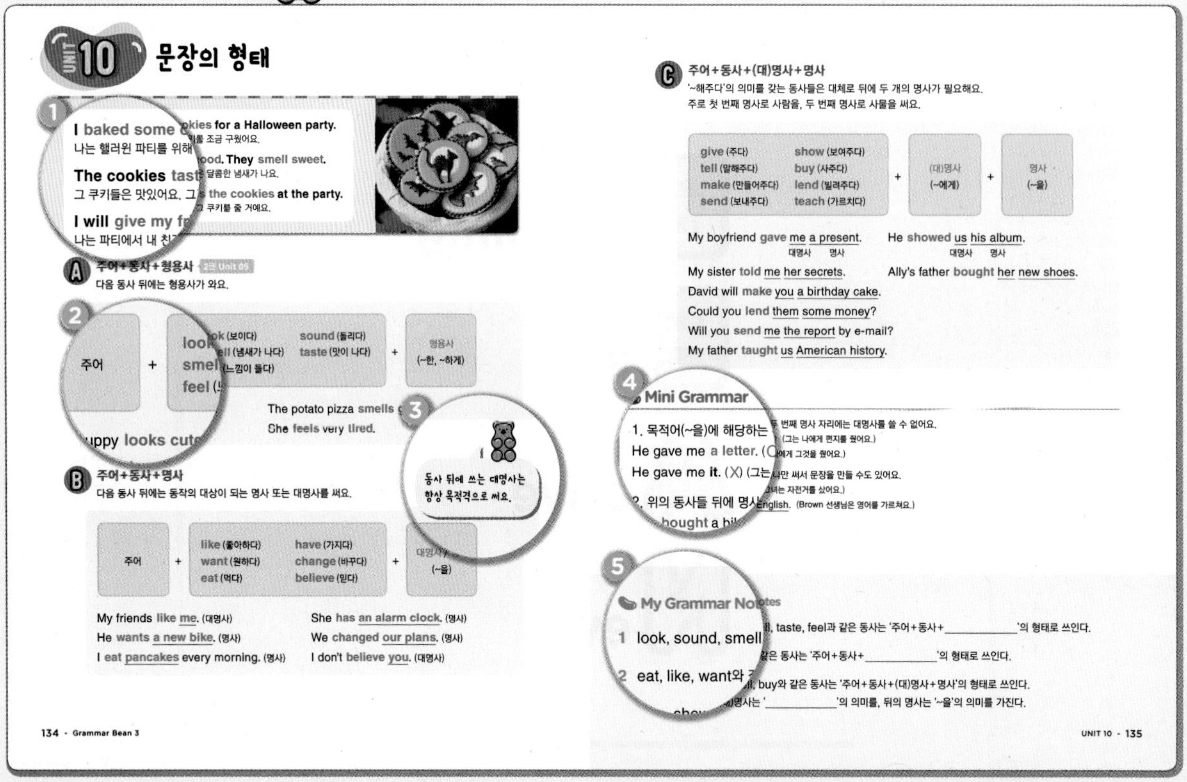

❶ 간단한 예문을 살펴보면서 학습할 내용을 예상해 보세요.

❷ 한눈에 들어오는 문법 정리와 예문으로 문법 내용을 쉽게 이해할 수 있어요.

❸ 말풍선 안에는 주의해야 하거나 꼭 기억해야 할 내용이 있으니 꼼꼼히 챙겨 보세요.

❹ Mini Grammar에서는 지금 공부하는 내용과 관련하여 추가적으로 알면 도움이 되는 문법 사항이 제시되어 있어요.

❺ My Grammar Notes는 학습한 내용을 정리하는 코너예요. 빈칸을 채우면서 요점을 정리해 보세요.

다양한 유형의 3단계 Exercise + Test

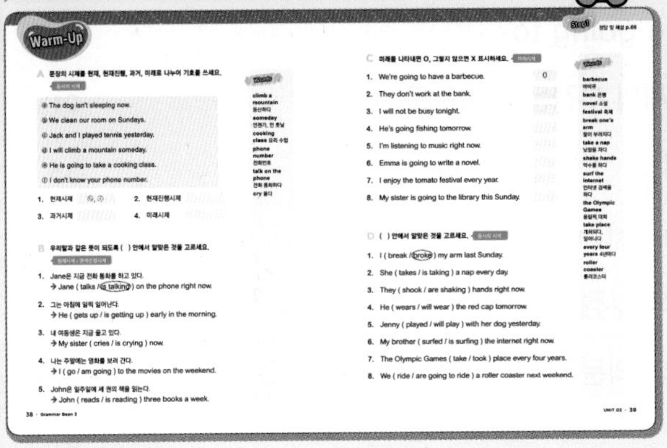

Warm-Up

새롭게 학습한 내용을 충분히 이해했나요? 간단한 문제를 통해 점검해 보세요.

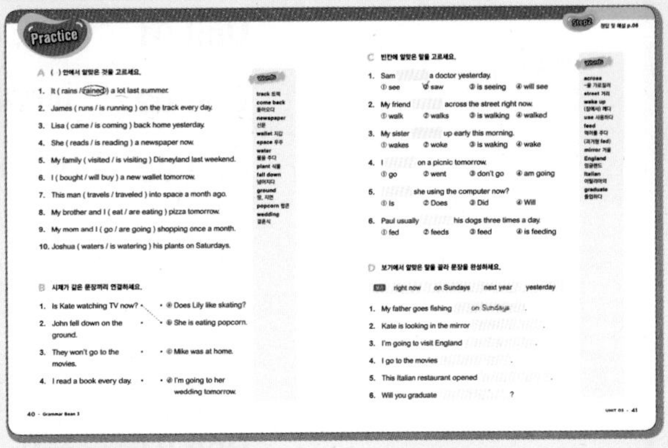

Practice

연습이 최선이라는 말 알고 있죠? 다양하고 많은 연습문제를 풀면서 자연스럽게 문법을 익힐 수 있어요.

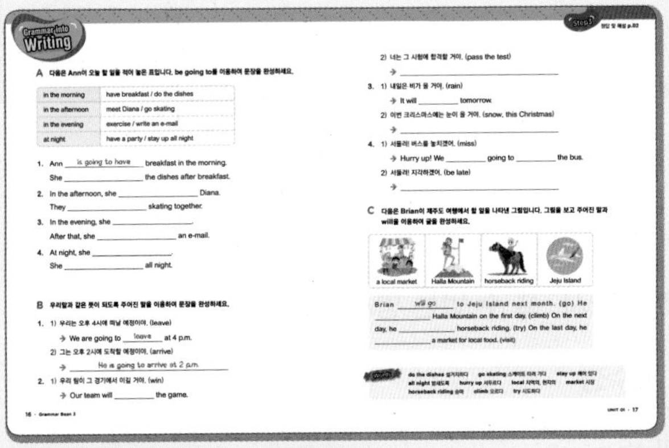

Grammar into Writing

문법을 배우는 목적이 문제 풀이와 시험만은 아니에요. 문법을 활용하면 영어 문장을 쓰는 것도 문제 없어요.

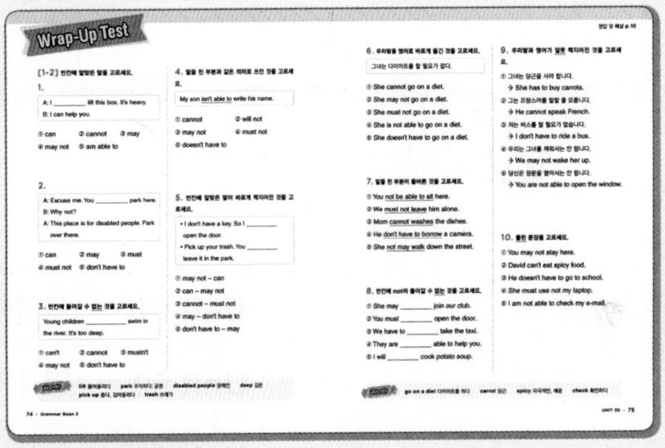

Wrap-Up Test

객관식 문제와 서술형 문제를 통해 배운 내용을 총정리해 보세요. 점수가 좋지 않으면 복습을 잊지 마세요.

+ Workbook

각 Unit별 연습문제와 별도의 Grammar Test가 수록되어 있어요.
Workbook을 통해 부족한 부분을 보충하고 배운 내용을 내 것으로 만들어 보세요.

CONTENTS

STUDY PLAN

차시	진도 현황 (교재)		숙제 (Workbook)	학습 날짜	복습 (O/X)	어휘 (전/후)
1차시	Unit 01	will, be going to		월 일		개 / 개
2차시				월 일		
3차시	Unit 02	미래시제의 부정문과 의문문		월 일		
4차시				월 일		
5차시	Unit 03	시제 비교		월 일		
6차시				월 일		
7차시	Unit 04	can, must, may		월 일		
8차시				월 일		
9차시	Unit 05	조동사의 부정문		월 일		
10차시				월 일		
11차시	Unit 06	조동사의 의문문		월 일		
12차시				월 일		
13차시	Unit 07	부사		월 일		
14차시				월 일		
15차시	Unit 08	빈도부사		월 일		
16차시				월 일		
17차시	Unit 09	숫자 표현		월 일		
18차시				월 일		
19차시	Unit 10	문장의 형태		월 일		
20차시				월 일		

❶ 숙제 칸에는 숙제 내용을 적고, 학습 날짜 칸에는 수업 날짜를 적어요.
❷ 오답 복습을 완료하면 복습 칸에 동그라미(O) 표시를 해요.
❸ 학습하기 전 모르는 어휘 개수를 칸 왼쪽에 적고, 학습 후 틀린 어휘 개수를 칸 오른쪽에 적어요.
(www.nebooks.co.kr에서 어휘 리스트를 받아 공부하세요!)

UNIT 01

will / be going to

Vocab Check! 이번 과에서 배울 단어의 뜻을 확인하고, 모르는 단어에 체크 표시하세요.

1	later	부 나중에	11	soon	부 곧	21	festival	명 축제
2	fight	동 싸우다	12	leave	동 떠나다	22	almost	부 거의
3	stay	동 머무르다	13	ill	형 아픈	23	storm	명 폭풍우
4	grade	명 학년	14	stay up	깨어 있다	24	all day	하루 종일
5	travel	동 여행하다	15	thirsty	형 목마른	25	try	동 시도하다
6	Europe	명 유럽	16	local	형 지역의, 현지의	26	climb	동 오르다
7	go on a picnic	소풍 가다	17	miss	동 놓치다	27	learn	동 배우다
8	attend	동 참석하다	18	dye	동 염색하다	28	join	동 참가하다
9	meeting	명 회의	19	sell	동 팔다	29	finish	동 끝내다
10	change	동 바꾸다	20	be good at	~을 잘하다	30	India	명 인도

UNIT 01

will, be going to

I love Superman.
저는 슈퍼맨을 사랑해요.

I will send a letter to him.
저는 그에게 편지를 보낼 거예요.

I am going to see his new movie.
저는 그의 새 영화를 볼 거예요.

A will, be going to

will 또는 be going to로 미래에 있을 일을 나타내요.

주어	+	will be going to	+	동사원형

B will+동사원형: ~할 것이다, ~하겠다

will은 미래에 대한 예측, 계획, 의지를 나타내요. will은 주어에 따라 모양이 바뀌지 않아요.

주어	+	will (~할 것이다)	+	**help** you. (당신을 도울) **be** angry. (화날)

I **will call** you tomorrow.

She **will be** 14 next year.

We **will go** camping this weekend.

They **will leave** the bus stop soon.

Mini Grammar

미래를 나타내는 표현

다음 표현들은 미래를 나타내므로 다음 표현들이 있을 때는 보통 동사 앞에 will이나 be going to를 써야 해요.

tomorrow (내일), **soon** (곧), **later** (나중에)

next ~ (다음 ~): next week (다음 주) / next month (다음 달) / next year (내년)

this ~ (이번 ~): this week (이번 주) / this month (이번 달) / this year (올해)

C be going to+동사원형: ~할 예정이다

be going to는 미래에 확정된 계획을 나타내요.

주어	+	am going to are going to is going to (~할 예정이다)	+	동사원형

I **am going to read** a book.

We **are going to dance** tonight.

She **is going to play** baseball after school.

Mini Grammar

대명사 주어+will의 줄임말

대명사 주어 뒤에 나오는 will은 주어 뒤에 'll로 줄여 쓸 수 있어요.

I will	⇨	I'll	I'll help you.
you will		you'll	You'll go to school.
he will		he'll	He'll watch TV soon.
she will		she'll	She'll be a good teacher.
it will		it'll	It'll be hot tomorrow.
we will		we'll	We'll clean the classroom.
they will		they'll	They'll visit us next week.

be going to의 be동사는 주어에 붙여서 줄여쓸 수 있어요.
I am going to → I'm going to
He is going to → He's going to
They are going to
→ They're going to

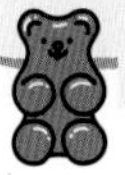

My Grammar Notes

1 미래시제는 앞으로 일어날 일이나 미래의 계획을 나타내는 말로 '~할 것이다'라는 의미이다.

2 미래를 나타내는 두 가지 방법

(1) __________ +동사원형: He __________ arrive soon.

(2) be동사+__________ __________ +동사원형: I am __________ __________ marry her.

Warm-Up

A 미래를 나타내는 문장에 V 표시하세요. will / be going to

1. They will go out for dinner. V
2. My father is going to go fishing.
3. He is going to school right now.
4. The baby is sleeping right now.
5. It will be sunny today.
6. I'll get up early tomorrow.
7. John fought with his brother last night.
8. I'm going to send you an e-mail soon.

Words

go out 외출하다
go fishing 낚시하러 가다
right now 지금 당장
sunny 화창한
get up 일어나다
early 일찍
fight 싸우다 (과거형 **fought**)
e-mail 이메일
busy 바쁜
grade 학년
stay 머무르다

B 빈칸에 알맞은 것을 연결하세요. will / be going to

1. Kate **was** busy yesterday. • • ⓐ will be
   Kate ______ busy now. • • ⓑ is
   Kate ______ busy tomorrow. • • ⓒ was

2. I ______ at home last week. • • ⓐ am staying
   I ______ at home now. • • ⓑ stayed
   I ______ at home next week. • • ⓒ am going to stay

3. He ______ 2nd grade last year. • • ⓐ teaches
   He ______ 4th grade this year. • • ⓑ will teach
   He ______ 6th grade next year. • • ⓒ taught

C will이 들어갈 위치에 V 표시하세요. will

1. It V snow tomorrow.
2. They go on a picnic.
3. She be a famous model.
4. The shop open next year.
5. We travel to Europe together.
6. He go swimming next Sunday.
7. There be a festival this Saturday.
8. My sister and I see a movie tonight.

Words

go on a picnic 소풍 가다
famous 유명한
travel 여행하다
Europe 유럽
festival 축제
invite 초대하다
see a doctor 진료를 받다
take a train 기차를 타다
move 이사하다

D 보기에서 알맞은 것을 골라 빈칸에 쓰세요. be going to

보기 am going to / are going to / is going to

1. I **am going to** meet his teacher.
2. She ______ buy a camera.
3. We ______ invite him to the party.
4. Amy ______ see a doctor.
5. Eric and Fred ______ take a train.
6. They ______ come to school at 9.
7. My uncle ______ move to Busan.
8. Many people ______ watch the soccer game.

Practice

A ( ) 안에서 알맞은 것을 고르세요.

1. It is going to (rain / rains).
2. They will (help / helping) us.
3. I'll (send / sending) you a postcard.
4. I will (made / make) spaghetti for you.
5. I'm (will / going to) change my hairstyle.
6. She will (is / be) in Canada next year.
7. He's going to (drinks / drink) coffee.
8. We are going to (attend / attending) the meeting.

Words

postcard 엽서
spaghetti 스파게티
change 바꾸다
hairstyle 머리 모양, 헤어스타일
attend 참석하다
meeting 회의
windy 바람이 부는
arrive 도착하다
Japanese 일본어
leave 떠나다

B 밑줄 친 부분을 줄임말로 바꿔 쓰세요.

1. It will be windy tomorrow. → It'll
2. You will arrive soon. →
3. I am going to buy a smartphone. →
4. He is going to study Japanese. →
5. She will be 15 years old next year. →
6. We are going to go to China. →
7. He will play the piano at the concert. →
8. They are going to leave tonight. →

C be동사를 알맞은 형태로 바꿔 쓰세요. 필요하면 will을 이용하세요.

1. Stay here. I will be back soon.
2. Eat some food. You ______ hungry later.
3. John ______ ill now. He ______ better soon.
4. I ______ at school now. I ______ home in an hour.
5. It ______ sunny today, but it ______ cloudy tomorrow.
6. Amelia ______ 12 years old last year. She ______ 14 next year.
7. We ______ not good at swimming. We ______ good swimmers after this class.

D be going to와 주어진 단어를 이용하여 빈칸에 알맞은 말을 쓰세요.

1. It is cold. I am going to turn on the heater. (turn)
2. We missed the bus. We ______ late. (be)
3. I'm making curry. I ______ lunch soon. (have)
4. I love this place. I ______ a picture here. (take)
5. Linda is going to the hair salon. She ______ her hair. (dye)
6. That baseball player is the best. He ______ a home run. (hit)

Words

be back 돌아오다
hungry 배고픈
later 나중에
ill 아픈
better 더 나은
in an hour 한 시간 뒤에
cloudy 흐린
be good at ~을 잘하다
swimming 수영
swimmer 수영선수
turn on (전원을) 켜다
heater 히터, 난방기
miss 놓치다
curry 카레
place 장소
take a picture 사진을 찍다
hair salon 미용실
hair 머리카락
dye 염색하다
home run 홈런
hit 치다

E will과 보기의 단어를 이용하여 빈칸에 알맞은 말을 쓰세요.

보기 meet go be pass drink close

1. It's raining. I **will close** the window.
2. Take it easy. You ________ the exam.
3. Don't be sad. We ________ each other again someday.
4. I'm thirsty. I ________ some water.
5. My brother is 7. He ________ to school next year.
6. Stay at home this weekend. It ________ cold and rainy.

F be going to와 보기의 단어를 이용하여 빈칸에 알맞은 말을 쓰세요.

보기 sell read fly make buy exercise

1. Jessica went shopping. She **is going to buy** a skirt.
2. She is sitting on a chair. She ________ a book.
3. It's almost 6 o'clock. Dad ________ dinner soon.
4. There is a bird in the tree. It ________ away soon.
5. There is a bazaar today. I ________ my old toys.
6. My brother and I got up early today. We ________ outside.

Words

pass (시험에) 통과하다
Take it easy 진정해. 걱정 마.
exam 시험
each other 서로
someday 언젠가
thirsty 목마른
weekend 주말
sell 팔다
exercise 운동하다
skirt 치마
almost 거의
bazaar 바자회
outside 밖에서

G 밑줄 친 부분을 바르게 고쳐 쓰세요.

1. We will are at home this evening. → will be
2. Jenny will gets a perm. →
3. They will going to wash their hands. →
4. It's going to rain. I will took an umbrella. →
5. He will is in Sydney next month. →
6. It's too late. I will going home. →
7. It will is cloudy this Wednesday. →
8. My father will buys a new car next year. →
9. There was a storm tomorrow. →
10. I missed the bus. I going to be late. →
11. We're going play baseball tomorrow. →
12. I am go to ride a bike this afternoon. →
13. She is going to reading English novels. →
14. They are going be scientists in the future. →
15. Julia is going to wears a new dress tonight. →
16. I'm going to sleeping all day this Sunday. →
17. I'm going give him a soccer ball. →
18. Steve and Billy is going to take some pictures. →

Words

get a perm 파마하다
umbrella 우산
Sydney (호주) 시드니
cloudy 흐린
storm 폭풍우
novel 소설
scientist 과학자
in the future 미래에
all day 하루 종일
soccer ball 축구공

Grammar into Writing

A **다음은 Ann이 오늘 할 일을 적어 놓은 표입니다. be going to를 이용하여 문장을 완성하세요.**

in the morning	have breakfast / do the dishes
in the afternoon	meet Diana / go skating
in the evening	exercise / write an e-mail
at night	have a party / stay up all night

1. Ann ___is going to have___ breakfast in the morning.

   She ____________________ the dishes after breakfast.

2. In the afternoon, she ____________________ Diana.

   They ____________________ skating together.

3. In the evening, she ____________________.

   After that, she ____________________ an e-mail.

4. At night, she ____________________.

   She ____________________ all night.

B **우리말과 같은 뜻이 되도록 주어진 말을 이용하여 문장을 완성하세요.**

1. 1) 우리는 오후 4시에 떠날 예정이야. (leave)

   → We are going to ___leave___ at 4 p.m.

   2) 그는 오후 2시에 도착할 예정이야. (arrive)

   → ___He is going to arrive at 2 p.m.___

2. 1) 우리 팀이 그 경기에서 이길 거야. (win)

   → Our team will __________ the game.

2) 너는 그 시험에 합격할 거야. (pass the test)

→ ______________________________

3. 1) 내일은 비가 올 거야. (rain)

→ It will __________ tomorrow.

2) 이번 크리스마스에는 눈이 올 거야. (snow, this Christmas)

→ ______________________________

4. 1) 서둘러! 버스를 놓치겠어. (miss)

→ Hurry up! We __________ going to __________ the bus.

2) 서둘러! 지각하겠어. (be late)

→ ______________________________

C 다음은 Brian이 제주도 여행에서 할 일을 나타낸 그림입니다. 그림을 보고 주어진 말과 will을 이용하여 글을 완성하세요.

Halla Mountain

a market

horseback riding

Jeju Island

Brian __will go to Jeju Island__ next month. (go to) He ____________ ____________ on the first day. (climb) On the next day, he ____________ ____________. (try) On the last day, he ____________________ for local food. (visit)

Words **do the dishes** 설거지하다 **go skating** 스케이트 타러 가다 **stay up** 깨어 있다 **all night** 밤새도록 **hurry up** 서두르다 **local** 지역의, 현지의 **market** 시장 **horseback riding** 승마 **climb** 오르다 **try** 시도하다

Wrap-Up Test

[1-2] 빈칸에 알맞은 말을 고르세요.

1.

My parents __________ going to travel to Egypt.

① be ② is
③ are ④ will
⑤ do

2.

He will ______________ the violin in the orchestra.

① play ② plays
③ playing ④ be going to play
⑤ played

3. 미래시제로 바꿀 때 will이 들어갈 위치로 알맞은 것을 고르세요.

They ① meet ② their ③ friends ④ in the theater ⑤.

4. 우리말을 영어로 바르게 옮긴 것을 고르세요.

나는 올해 태권도를 배울 것이다.

① I learn taekwondo this year.
② I learned taekwondo this year.
③ I will learn taekwondo this year.
④ I am going learn taekwondo this year.
⑤ I am go to learn taekwondo this year.

5. 다음 문장에서 틀린 부분을 바르게 고친 것을 고르세요.

She will bought a new camera tomorrow.

① will → is going
② bought → buy
③ a new → new a
④ tomorrow → yesterday
⑤ a new camera → new camera

Words **parents** 부모님 **Egypt** 이집트 **orchestra** 오케스트라, 관현악단 **theater** 극장 **learn** 배우다 **taekwondo** 태권도

6. 빈칸에 알맞은 말이 바르게 짝지어진 것을 고르세요.

Bill and Kate ________ in Spain now.
They ________ in Korea next year.

① are – were
② are – will be
③ will be – are
④ will be – will be
⑤ were – will be

7. 밑줄 친 부분의 의미가 다른 것을 고르세요.

① We are going to move this weekend.
② He is going to join the baseball team.
③ She is going to the park now.
④ I'm going to finish my homework this afternoon.
⑤ They're going to arrive at 7 p.m.

8. 밑줄 친 부분이 어색한 것을 고르세요.

① He will bring his laptop.
② They will be 13 next year.
③ I am going to have some milk.
④ The baby is going to sleep soon.
⑤ It will be going to snow later.

9. 빈칸에 들어갈 수 없는 것을 고르세요.

She will go to India ____________.

① this weekend
② last night
③ next month
④ tomorrow
⑤ tonight

10. 올바른 문장을 고르세요.

① I am going see a doctor.
② The soccer game will starts at 6 p.m.
③ Richard is going to has lunch soon.
④ Amy and Tom will going to be late.
⑤ We're going to stay at home this weekend.

Words **join** 참가하다 **team** 팀 **finish** 끝내다 **laptop** 노트북 컴퓨터 **India** 인도

11. 빈칸에 들어갈 말이 나머지와 다른 것을 고르세요.

① Dave will _________ a singer.

② He _________ going to the zoo soon.

③ She _________ going to clean her room in the evening.

④ My sister _________ a high school student.

⑤ It _________ going to rain later.

서술형

12. 빈칸에 알맞은 말을 쓰세요.

Her brothers _________ _________ _________ visit her next week.

서술형

13. 틀린 부분을 찾아 바르게 고쳐 쓰세요.

The library will closes late next month.

_________ → _________

14. 다음 문장을 일어난 순서대로 배열하세요.

① I'm eating the cake at the moment.

② I will make a chocolate cake tomorrow.

③ I made a cheesecake yesterday.

_________ → _________ → _________

서술형

15. 우리말과 같은 뜻이 되도록 주어진 말을 바르게 배열하세요.

나는 올해 크리스마스 카드를 만들 것이다.

(am / make / I / to / going / Christmas cards)

→ _________________________________

_________________________________ this year.

Words **high school** 고등학교 **library** 도서관 **at the moment** 바로 지금 **cheesecake** 치즈케이크

UNIT 02

미래시제의 부정문과 의문문

Vocab Check! 이번 과에서 배울 단어의 뜻을 확인하고, 모르는 단어에 체크 표시하세요.

☑ 1 swing 명 그네	11 on time 정시에	21 again 부 다시
2 participate 동 참가하다	12 anymore 부 더 이상	22 aquarium 명 수족관
3 farmer 명 농부	13 job 명 일, 직업	23 take care of ~을 돌보다
4 win 동 이기다	14 vegetable 명 채소	24 mind 명 마음
5 truth 명 진실	15 pay 동 지불하다	25 forgive 동 용서하다
6 brunch 명 아침 겸 점심	16 quiet 형 조용한	26 tired 형 피곤한
7 present 명 선물	17 trust 동 믿다	27 mistake 명 실수
8 post office 명 우체국	18 lend 동 빌려주다	28 see a doctor 진찰 받다
9 tell a lie 거짓말하다	19 grow 동 기르다, 재배하다	29 subway 명 지하철
10 sign up 등록하다, 신청하다	20 special 형 특별한	30 keep a secret 비밀을 지키다

UNIT 02 미래시제의 부정문과 의문문

Julie and I will go to the amusement park.
Julie와 나는 놀이공원에 갈 거예요.

I will not ride a roller coaster.
나는 롤러코스터를 타지 않을 거예요.

Is she going to ride it?
그녀는 롤러코스터를 탈까요?

A 미래시제의 부정문: ~(하지) 않을 것이다

미래형의 부정문은 will 뒤와 be going to의 be 뒤에 not을 붙여 나타내요.

1. will의 부정문

will 뒤에 not을 붙여 'will not+동사원형'으로 나타내요.

주어	+	will not (= won't) (~ 않을 것이다)	+	동사원형

They **will** go to the library.
⇨ They **will not** go to the library.
= They **won't** go to the library.

2. be going to의 부정문

be동사 뒤에 not을 써서 'be not going to+동사원형'으로 나타내요.

주어	+	am / are / is	not going to	+	동사원형

(~ 않을 것이다)

I **am going to** play outside.
⇨ I **am not going to** play outside.
We **are going to** watch the show.
⇨ We**'re not going to** watch the show.

B 미래시제의 의문문: ~할 거니? ~할 예정이니?

미래형의 의문문은 will과 be going to의 be를 주어 앞으로 옮겨 만들어요.

1. will의 의문문

will을 주어 앞으로 옮겨 'Will+주어+동사원형 ~?'으로 나타내요.

질문		
Will (~할 건가요?)	주어	**동사원형** ~?

➔

대답
Yes, 주어+**will**. (네, 그럴 거예요.)
No, 주어+**won't**. (아니요, 안 그럴 거예요.)

She **will** attend the meeting.

➔ **Will she** attend the meeting?

– **Yes**, she **will**. / **No**, she **won't**.

2. be going to의 의문문

be동사를 주어 앞으로 옮겨 'be+주어+going to+동사원형 ~?'으로 나타내요.

질문			
Am / **Are** / **Is**	주어	**going to**	**동사원형** ~?
~할 건가요?			

➔

대답
Yes, 주어+**be**동사. (네, 그럴 거예요.)
No, 주어+**be**동사+**not**. (아니요, 안 그럴 거예요.)

They **are going to** sell the house.

➔ **Are they going to** sell the house?

– **Yes**, they **are**. / **No**, they **aren't**.

My Grammar Notes

1 will의 부정문: 주어+__________+__________+동사원형 (will not = __________)
will의 의문문: __________+주어+동사원형 ~?

2 be going to의 부정문: 주어+be동사+__________+going to+동사원형
be going to의 의문문: be동사+주어+__________ __________+동사원형 ~?

Warm-Up

A not이 들어갈 수 있는 위치에 V 표시하세요. 미래시제의 부정문

1. I will V join the club.
2. My sister will go to bed early.
3. You will pass the driver's test.
4. We will have a party tonight.
5. The kids are going to play on the swings.
6. I am going to take a bus.
7. They are going to go for a walk.
8. The girl is going to wash her hands.

Words

join 가입하다
driver's test 운전시험
swing 그네
go for a walk 산책하러 가다
dentist 치과 의사
letter 편지
leave 떠나다
answer the phone 전화를 받다
stay up 깨어 있다

B 밑줄 친 부분을 줄여 쓰세요. 미래시제의 부정문

1. It will not be cold tomorrow. → It won't
2. I am not going to play tennis. →
3. She is not going to see the dentist. →
4. I will not read the letter. →
5. They are not going to meet her. →
6. Jack is not going to leave. →
7. He will not answer the phone. →
8. Eric will not stay up late. →

C ( ) 안에서 알맞은 것을 고르세요. 미래시제의 의문문

1. (Will / Is) she going to go with him?
2. (Will / Are) your friends go to the concert?
3. (Will / Am) I going to win this game?
4. (Will / Are) you going to tell the truth?
5. (Will / Are) Mr. and Mrs. Smith come today?
6. (Will / Is) Sujin going to visit Boston?

Words

win 이기다
truth 진실
visit 방문하다
Boston (미국) 보스턴
again 다시
for long 오랫동안
present 선물
grocery store 식품점, 슈퍼마켓

D 빈칸에 알맞은 말을 쓰세요. 미래시제의 의문문

1. Will he call me again?
   – No, he won't.
2. Will Mark and Alice come for dinner this evening?
   – Yes, ______ ______.
3. Are you going to stay in the country for long?
   – Yes, ______ ______.
4. Is Emily going to give him a present?
   – Yes, ______ ______.
5. Is your father going to drive you to school?
   – No, ______ ______.
6. Will you go to the grocery store with me?
   – No, ______ ______.

Practice

A ( ) 안에서 알맞은 것을 고르세요.

1. I (will not / not will) eat fast food.
2. It won't (rain / rains) this weekend.
3. We won't (stay / to stay) in Hong Kong.
4. She (doesn't / isn't) going to wear glasses.
5. They're not going to (work / works) tonight.
6. I'm not going to (invite / inviting) him to the party.
7. They (won't / aren't) participate in the bazaar.

Words

weekend 주말
wear glasses 안경을 쓰다
invite 초대하다
participate 참가하다
bazaar 바자회
bookstore 서점

B 빈칸에 알맞은 말을 써서 대화를 완성하세요.

1. Am I going to see you again?
   – Yes, you are.
2. ______ ______ buy a new car?
   – No, she won't.
3. Will he be 20 years old next year?
   – ______, ______ ______. He will be 22.
4. ______ Minsu going to go to the bookstore?
   – Yes, ______ ______.
5. ______ you going to make a Christmas cake?
   – No, ______ ______.

C will과 주어진 단어를 이용하여 빈칸에 알맞은 말을 쓰세요.

1.	not / call	I won't call him.
2.	not / meet	We ______ Dan tomorrow.
3.	study	Leo ______ at the library.
4.	not / win	They ______ the game.
5.	take	Kelly ______ the test.
6.	not / be	Lucy ______ there on time.
7.	have	I ______ brunch with him.
8.	not / speak	My mom ______ to him anymore.

Words

library 도서관
take a test 시험을 치다
on time 정시에
brunch 아침 겸 점심
anymore 더 이상
Rome (이탈리아) 로마
job 일, 직업
ticket 티켓, 표
pay 지불하다
in cash 현금으로
quiet 조용한
take a bus 버스를 타다

D be going to와 주어진 단어를 이용하여 빈칸에 알맞은 말을 쓰세요.

1.	not / visit	I am not going to visit Rome next month.
2.	not / stay	The man ______ long.
3.	get	He ______ a new job.
4.	not / eat	We ______ dinner today.
5.	buy	She ______ the ticket.
6.	not / pay	They ______ in cash.
7.	not / be	The children ______ quiet.
8.	take	Karen ______ a bus to the park.

E will 또는 be going to와 주어진 단어를 이용하여 대화를 완성하세요.

1. Will the class start next week? (the class, start)
   – Yes, it will. It will begin next Monday.

2. ________ your friend in Paris? (meet)
   – Yes, I am. I'm going to stay at his house for two days.

3. ________ a secret? (keep)
   – Yes, they will. I trust them.

4. ________ soon? (the train, leave)
   – No, it isn't. It won't leave until 8.

5. ________ Korean? (Rachel, learn)
   – Yes, she is. She signed up for Korean classes.

6. ________ me? (marry)
   – Yes, I will. I love you.

7. ________ the car to me tomorrow? (lend)
   – No, I won't. I am going to use it.

8. ________ a bus? (take)
   – No, he isn't. He's going to take a taxi.

9. ________ a birthday present to Sally? (give)
   – Yes, we are. We'll give her a special present.

10. ________ at 7 p.m.? (the concert, end)
   – No, it isn't. It is going to end at 8 p.m.

Words

start 시작하다
keep a secret 비밀을 지키다
trust 믿다
until ~까지
sign up 등록하다, 신청하다
marry 결혼하다
lend 빌려주다
special 특별한
end 끝나다

F 밑줄 친 부분을 바르게 고쳐 쓰세요.

1. We won't are late again. → be
2. It not will snow tomorrow. →
3. She won't not sell the house. →
4. We not going to visit the aquarium. →
5. My parents are going not to go there. →
6. Does she call me back later? →
7. Does he going to buy a new shirt? →
8. Are the baby going to sleep? →
9. He is not go to stay in Italy. →
10. Will buy you a new smartphone? →
11. Will she makes kimchi this weekend? →
12. Will they remember us? – No, they don't. →
13. Are they going to go skiing this Sunday?
– Yes, they aren't. →
14. Will Mr. Brown change his mind?
– Yes, he is. →
15. Are you going to see Lisa tonight?
– No, we won't. →
16. Will you take a shower after dinner?
– Yes, I am. →

Words

sell 팔다
aquarium 수족관
call ~ back ~에게 다시 전화하다
Italy 이탈리아
remember 기억하다
go skiing 스키 타러 가다
change 바꾸다
mind 마음
take a shower 샤워하다

Grammar into Writing

A 다음 표를 보고, 주어진 말을 이용하여 대화를 완성하세요.

Friday	Saturday	Sunday	Monday
 snowy	 rainy	 sunny	 cloudy

A: Will it be sunny on Friday?
B: No, __it__ __won't__. It will be __snowy__.
A: Will it be snowy on Saturday?
B: ________, ________ ________. It ________ ________ ________.
A: How about Sunday? I'm going to take a drive.
B: It ________ ________ sunny. But I'm sad.
A: What's wrong?
B: My class is going to go on a picnic on Monday. It's ________ ________ ________ ________.
A: Oh, that's too bad.

B 우리말과 같은 뜻이 되도록 주어진 말을 이용하여 문장을 만드세요.

1. 그는 오늘 세차를 하지 않을 것이다. be going to / wash his car
→ __He isn't going to wash his car today.__

2. 너는 Kelly의 생일 파티에 갈 거니? will / go to Kelly's birthday party
→ ________________________________

3. 너는 초콜릿을 살 거니? be going to / buy some chocolate

→ ______________________________

4. 나는 전화를 받지 않을 것이다. be going to / answer the phone

→ ______________________________

5. 나는 Brad와 점심을 먹지 않을 것이다. will / have lunch with Brad

→ ______________________________

6. 너는 그를 용서해 줄 거니? will / forgive him

→ ______________________________

C 다음은 소라의 현재 상태와 앞으로의 결심을 나타낸 글입니다. will과 won't를 써서 소라의 변화를 나타내는 글을 쓰세요.

Sora does...

1. She doesn't exercise every day.
2. She doesn't read a lot of books.
3. She doesn't study hard.
4. She doesn't clean her room.
5. She tells lies.
6. She gets up late.
7. She fights with her sister.

Sora will...

1. She will exercise every day.
2. ______________________
3. ______________________
4. ______________________
5. ______________________
6. ______________________
7. ______________________

Words **take a drive** 드라이브하다 **wrong** 잘못된 **forgive** 용서하다 **tell a lie** 거짓말하다 **fight** 싸우다

Wrap-Up Test

1. 미래를 나타내는 문장을 고르세요.

① He wasn't tired at all.

② He didn't finish his work.

③ Steve works at the post office.

④ She isn't listening to him right now.

⑤ I'm not going to see a doctor later.

[2-3] 빈칸에 알맞은 말을 고르세요.

2.

Will they __________ care of the cat?

① take ② taking

③ took ④ takes

⑤ be going to take

3.

She is not going to __________ her parents next week.

① visits ② visit

③ visiting ④ visited

⑤ will visit

4. 부정문으로 바꿀 때 빈칸에 알맞은 것을 고르세요.

He will pass the driver's test tomorrow. → He __________ pass the driver's test tomorrow.

① isn't ② don't

③ doesn't ④ didn't

⑤ won't

5. not이 들어갈 위치가 잘못 표시된 것을 고르세요.

① He is ∨ going to go fishing.

② She will ∨ go with you.

③ I will ∨ make a sandwich for you.

④ They are going ∨ to stay in a hotel.

⑤ You're ∨ going to call me again.

Words **(not) at all** 전혀 **tired** 피곤한 **post office** 우체국 **see a doctor** 진찰 받다 **take care of** ~을 돌보다

6. 빈칸에 알맞은 말이 바르게 짝지어진 것을 고르세요.

A: _________ you be free this afternoon?
B: Yes, I will. Why?
A: We _________ going to play basketball. Let's go together.

① Will – will
② Are – are
③ Will – are
④ Are – will
⑤ Do – are

7. 빈칸에 들어갈 말이 나머지와 다른 것을 고르세요.

① _________ you going to be 13 years old next year?
② They _________ not going to drink coffee at night.
③ _________ the boys going to swim in the sea?
④ Mary and her sister _________ not ride bikes tomorrow.
⑤ We _________ not going to play baseball next week.

8. 틀린 문장을 고르세요.

① Will she come again?
② I won't make mistakes.
③ Is she going to keep the dog?
④ He is not going to leave yesterday.
⑤ They'll not invite you to the party.

9. 빈칸에 won't를 쓸 수 없는 것을 고르세요.

① She _________ sing the song.
② I _________ not join the dance club.
③ My father _________ be here tomorrow.
④ They _________ take the subway.
⑤ Diana _________ win the game.

10. 우리말을 영어로 바르게 옮긴 것을 고르세요.

그들은 내일 영화를 보지 않을 것이다.

① They are not watch a movie tomorrow.
② They did not watch a movie tomorrow.
③ They won't watch a movie tomorrow.
④ They will watch a movie tomorrow.
⑤ They're going not to watch a movie tomorrow.

Words **free** 한가한 **sea** 바다 **ride** 타다 **mistake** 실수 **keep** 유지하다; 기르다 **dance club** 댄스 동아리 **subway** 지하철

11. 대화가 <u>어색한</u> 것을 고르세요.

① A: Are you going to go to Disneyland?
  B: Yes, we are.

② A: Will you help me with my homework?
  B: No, I won't.

③ A: Is Paul going to cook for us?
  B: No, he wasn't.

④ A: Will it rain this weekend?
  B: Yes, it will.

⑤ A: Will the mails arrive soon?
  B: No, they will not.

[12-13] 질문에 대한 대답으로 빈칸에 알맞은 말을 쓰세요.

서술형

12.

Are you going to buy a scarf for your mother?

– __________, __________ __________.

I'll buy some flowers for her.

서술형

13.

Will it snow on Friday?

– __________, __________ __________.

I will make a snowman outside.

서술형

14. <u>틀린</u> 부분을 찾아 바르게 고쳐 쓰세요.

The farmers not going to grow vegetables next year.

→ ______________________________

____

서술형

15. 우리말과 같은 뜻이 되도록 주어진 말을 바르게 배열하세요.

Ted는 일찍 오지 않을 것이다.
(Ted / will / come early / not)

→ ______________________________

Words mail 편지 arrive 도착하다 scarf 스카프 snowman 눈사람 farmer 농부 grow 기르다, 재배하다 vegetable 채소

UNIT 03

시제 비교

Vocab Check! 이번 과에서 배울 단어의 뜻을 확인하고, 모르는 단어에 체크 표시하세요.

1	bank	명 은행	11	England	명 잉글랜드	21	fall down	넘어지다
2	space	명 우주	12	practice	동 연습하다	22	shocking	형 충격적인
3	water	동 물을 주다	13	gym	명 체육관	23	jump rope	줄넘기하다
4	wallet	명 지갑	14	recently	부 최근에	24	novel	명 소설
5	ground	명 땅, 지면	15	employee	명 직원, 종업원	25	sunglasses	명 선글라스
6	wedding	명 결혼식	16	celebrate	동 기념하다, 축하하다	26	barbecue	명 바비큐
7	street	명 거리	17	costume	명 복장	27	feed	동 먹이를 주다
8	wake up	(잠에서) 깨다	18	neighbor	명 이웃	28	take a nap	낮잠을 자다
9	use	동 사용하다	19	race	명 경주, 달리기 (시합)	29	someday	부 언젠가, 먼 훗날
10	mirror	명 거울	20	graduate	동 졸업하다	30	these days	요즘에는

UNIT 03 시제 비교

I played a computer game yesterday.
나는 어제 컴퓨터 게임을 했어요.

I'm taking a math test now.
나는 지금 수학 시험을 보고 있어요.

It is too difficult. I will study hard.
그건 너무 어려워요. 나는 공부를 열심히 할 거예요.

A 과거 *vs.* 현재 *vs.* 미래

지금까지 배웠던 여러 가지 시제(현재시제, 현재진행시제, 과거시제, 미래시제)를 비교해 봅시다.

과거 (~였다, ~했다)	I **walked** home in the rain yesterday. (나는 어제 빗속에서 집으로 걸어왔어요.)
↓	↓
현재 (~이다, ~하다)	I **have** a bad cold now. (나는 지금 심한 감기에 걸렸어요.)
↓	↓
미래 (~일 것이다, ~할 것이다)	I **will see** a doctor tomorrow. (나는 내일 진찰을 받을 거예요.)

1. be동사의 과거, 현재, 미래

과거	was / were	She **was** a singer. (그녀는 가수였어요.)
현재	am / are / is	She **is** a singer. (그녀는 가수예요.)
미래	will be / be going to be	She **will be** a singer. (그녀는 가수가 될 거예요.)

2. 일반동사의 과거, 현재, 미래

과거	ran	He **ran** fast. (그는 빨리 달렸어요.)
현재	run	He **runs** fast. (그는 빨리 달려요.)
미래	will run / be going to run	He **will run** fast. (그는 빨리 달릴 거예요.)

B 현재 *vs.* 현재진행

일반동사의 현재형은 '~이다', '~하다'의 의미로, 지속적인 사실이나 상태, 혹은 반복되는 습관을 나타낼 때 써요.
일반동사의 현재진행형은 '~하는 중이다'의 의미로, 말하는 시점에 진행 중인 일을 나타내요.

현재시제	동사의 현재형	every day (매일), on Sundays (일요일마다), every Thursday (목요일마다)
현재진행시제	be동사+동사원형-ing	now (지금), right now (지금 당장)

Kids **love** donuts. (지속적인 사실)
He **wakes** up late **on Sundays.** (반복되는 습관)
Joe **is watching** TV **now.** (현재 진행 중인 일)

C 현재진행 *vs.* 미래

미래를 나타내는 방법에는 두 가지가 있어요.

1. will 또는 be going to 사용하기

I **will go** camping with my friends.
Susan **is going to clean** her room.

2. 현재진행형과 미래를 나타내는 말 같이 쓰기

He **is leaving** Korea **tomorrow**.
Are you **having** pizza **tonight**?

현재진행형은 미래를 나타내는 말과 함께 쓰여 가까운 미래에 예정되어 있는 일을 나타내기도 해요.

My Grammar Notes

1 동사는 과거, 현재, 미래의 시간을 나타낼 때 각각 다른 형태를 가진다.
play (놀다) → 현재: play(s) / 과거: ____________ / 미래: ____________, be going to play

2 현재시제는 지속적 사실이나 반복되는 습관을 나타내고, ____________(be동사+동사원형-ing)은 말하는 순간에 발생하고 있는 일을 나타낸다.

3 미래를 나타낼 때는 주로 will 또는 be ____________ to를 이용하지만, ____________을 이용하여 가까운 미래에 예정된 일을 나타내기도 한다.

Warm-Up

A 문장의 시제를 현재, 현재진행, 과거, 미래로 나누어 기호를 쓰세요.

동사의 시제

ⓐ The dog isn't sleeping now.

ⓑ We clean our room on Sundays.

ⓒ Jack and I played tennis yesterday.

ⓓ I will climb a mountain someday.

ⓔ He is going to take a cooking class.

ⓕ I don't know your phone number.

1. 현재시제 ⓑ, ⓕ　　**2.** 현재진행시제

3. 과거시제　　**4.** 미래시제

B 우리말과 같은 뜻이 되도록 (　) 안에서 알맞은 것을 고르세요.

현재시제 / 현재진행시제

1. Jane은 지금 전화 통화를 하고 있다.
→ Jane (talks / is talking) on the phone right now.

2. 그는 아침에 일찍 일어난다.
→ He (gets up / is getting up) early in the morning.

3. 내 여동생은 지금 울고 있다.
→ My sister (cries / is crying) now.

4. 나는 주말에는 영화를 보러 간다.
→ I (go / am going) to the movies on the weekend.

5. John은 일주일에 세 권의 책을 읽는다.
→ John (reads / is reading) three books a week.

Words

climb a mountain 등산하다
someday 언젠가, 먼 훗날
cooking class 요리 수업
phone number 전화번호
talk on the phone 전화 통화하다
cry 울다

C 미래를 나타내면 O, 그렇지 않으면 X 표시하세요. 미래시제

1. We're going to have a barbecue. O
2. They don't work at the bank.
3. I will not be busy tonight.
4. He's going fishing tomorrow.
5. I'm listening to music right now.
6. Emma is going to write a novel.
7. I enjoy the tomato festival every year.
8. My sister is going to the library this Sunday.

D ( ) 안에서 알맞은 것을 고르세요. 동사의 시제

1. I (break / broke) my arm last Sunday.
2. She (takes / is taking) a nap every day.
3. They (shook / are shaking) hands right now.
4. He (wears / will wear) the red cap tomorrow.
5. Jenny (played / will play) with her dog yesterday.
6. My brother (surfed / is surfing) the internet right now.
7. The Olympic Games (take / took) place every four years.
8. We (ride / are going to ride) a roller coaster next weekend.

Words

barbecue 바비큐
bank 은행
novel 소설
festival 축제
break one's arm 팔이 부러지다
take a nap 낮잠을 자다
shake hands 악수를 하다
surf the internet 인터넷 검색을 하다
the Olympic Games 올림픽 대회
take place 개최되다, 일어나다
every four years 4년마다
roller coaster 롤러코스터

Practice

A ( ) 안에서 알맞은 것을 고르세요.

1. It (rains / rained) a lot last summer.
2. James (runs / is running) on the track every day.
3. Lisa (came / is coming) back home yesterday.
4. She (reads / is reading) a newspaper now.
5. My family (visited / is visiting) Disneyland last weekend.
6. I (bought / will buy) a new wallet tomorrow.
7. This man (travels / traveled) into space a month ago.
8. My brother and I (eat / are eating) pizza tomorrow.
9. My mom and I (go / are going) shopping once a month.
10. Joshua (waters / is watering) his plants on Saturdays.

Words

track 트랙
come back 돌아오다
newspaper 신문
wallet 지갑
space 우주
water 물을 주다
plant 식물
fall down 넘어지다
ground 땅, 지면
popcorn 팝콘
wedding 결혼식

B 시제가 같은 문장끼리 연결하세요.

1. Is Kate watching TV now? • • ⓐ Does Lily like skating?
2. John fell down on the ground. • • ⓑ She is eating popcorn.
3. They won't go to the movies. • • ⓒ Mike was at home.
4. I read a book every day. • • ⓓ I'm going to her wedding tomorrow.

C 빈칸에 알맞은 말을 고르세요.

1. Sam ______ a doctor yesterday.
   ① see ② saw ③ is seeing ④ will see

2. My friend ______ across the street right now.
   ① walk ② walks ③ is walking ④ walked

3. My sister ______ up early this morning.
   ① wakes ② woke ③ is waking ④ wake

4. I ______ on a picnic tomorrow.
   ① go ② went ③ don't go ④ am going

5. ______ she using the computer now?
   ① Is ② Does ③ Did ④ Will

6. Paul usually ______ his dogs three times a day.
   ① fed ② feeds ③ feed ④ is feeding

Words

across ~을 가로질러
street 거리
wake up (잠에서) 깨다
use 사용하다
feed 먹이를 주다 (과거형 **fed**)
mirror 거울
England 잉글랜드
Italian 이탈리아의
graduate 졸업하다

D 보기에서 알맞은 말을 골라 문장을 완성하세요.

보기 right now on Sundays next year yesterday

1. My father goes fishing on Sundays.
2. Kate is looking in the mirror ______.
3. I'm going to visit England ______.
4. I go to the movies ______.
5. This Italian restaurant opened ______.
6. Will you graduate ______?

E 보기에서 알맞은 동사를 골라 시제에 맞게 바꿔 쓰세요.

보기 jump eat be practice take visit read

1. Joan jumped rope last night.
2. Next year I ____________ Japan.
3. Alex ____________ spaghetti yesterday.
4. James ____________ a comic book now.
5. He ____________ taekwondo at the gym right now.
6. Recently, she ____________ a shower in the morning.
7. The new employee ____________ late for work these days.

Words

jump rope 줄넘기하다
practice 연습하다
taekwondo 태권도
gym 체육관
recently 최근에
employee 직원, 종업원
these days 요즘에는
go on a field trip 견학 가다
still 아직(도)
have a party 파티를 열다

F 밑줄 친 부분을 바르게 고쳐 쓰세요.

1. He <u>are traveling</u> to Hong Kong. → is traveling
2. It <u>won't going to</u> rain tomorrow. → ____________
3. I <u>did not eating</u> breakfast yesterday. → ____________
4. We <u>went</u> on a field trip next Monday. → ____________
5. My sister <u>plays</u> with her cat right now. → ____________
6. Janet <u>leaves</u> the classroom ten minutes ago. → ____________
7. We still <u>had</u> a party on Mom's birthday every year. → ____________

G 부사에 맞게 알맞은 시제로 문장을 고쳐 쓰세요.

1. Tim writes e-mails every Wednesday.
   → Tim wrote e-mails yesterday.

2. We don't watch TV at night.
   → ______ right now.

3. Are you wearing new jeans now? (will 사용)
   → ______ tomorrow?

4. Dad cooked dinner for us last Sunday.
   → ______ now.

5. Jennifer is helping her mother now.
   → ______ yesterday.

6. This bakery opened last week. (be going to 사용)
   → ______ next week.

7. They will sing and dance tonight.
   → ______ last night.

8. My family moved to Seoul last month. (현재진행형 사용)
   → ______ next month.

9. He closed the window a few minutes ago.
   → ______ now.

10. Does she go scuba diving every summer?
    → ______ last year?

Words

at night 밤에
jeans 청바지
bakery 빵집
go scuba diving 스쿠버 다이빙하러 가다

Grammar into Writing

A 우리말과 같은 뜻이 되도록 보기와 주어진 말을 이용하여 문장을 만드세요.

보기 take do watch sell lose

1. 그는 몇 시간 전에 우산을 잃어버렸다. (his umbrella, a few hours ago)

   → He lost his umbrella a few hours ago.

2. 너는 지금 숙제를 하는 중이니? (your homework, now)

   → ______________________

3. John은 그 차를 팔지 않을 것이다. (going to, the car)

   → ______________________

4. 우리는 매주 월요일에 영어 시험을 본다. (an English test, every Monday)

   → ______________________

5. 너는 어젯밤에 그 경기를 봤니? (the game, last night)

   → ______________________

B 우리말과 같은 뜻이 되도록 주어진 말을 이용하여 문장을 완성하세요.

1. 1) 나는 아침마다 내 강아지와 함께 산책을 한다. (take)

   → I take a walk with my puppy every morning.

   2) Daniel은 주말마다 수영장에 간다. (go to the pool, on weekends)

   → Daniel goes to the pool on weekends.

2. 1) Betty와 Jack은 지금 축구를 하고 있다. (play)

   → Betty and Jack ________ ________ soccer now.

2) Joe는 지금 전화 통화를 하고 있는 중이다. (talk on the phone)

→ ______________________________

3\. 1) 너는 어제 네 컴퓨터를 고쳤니? (fix)

→ ________ you ________ your computer yesterday?

2) 그녀는 어제 등산하러 갔니? (go hiking)

→ ______________________________

4\. 1) 나는 내일 세차를 할 것이다. (wash)

→ I'm ________ ________ ________ my car tomorrow.

2) Katie는 내일 머리를 자를 것이다. (get a haircut)

→ ______________________________

C 다음 글을 읽고, 밑줄 친 부분을 바르게 고쳐 쓰세요.

Today is Halloween! My family ❶ is celebrating Halloween every year. I ❷ will wear a Dracula costume right now. My brother and I ❸ visit neighbors and asked for candy last year. We ❹ made a jack-o'-lantern next year.

↓

❶ celebrates ❷ ________________

❸ ________________ ❹ ________________

Words

get a haircut 머리를 자르다 **Halloween** 핼러윈 **celebrate** 기념하다, 축하하다 **Dracula** 드라큘라 **costume** 복장 **neighbor** 이웃 **ask for** 요구하다 **jack-o'-lantern** 호박 등

Wrap-Up Test

1. 빈칸에 알맞은 말을 고르세요.

I __________ this medicine yesterday.

① take ② took
③ am taking ④ will take
⑤ takes

2. 빈칸에 들어갈 수 없는 것을 고르세요.

They will run a race __________.

① soon ② next Friday
③ tomorrow ④ next month
⑤ an hour ago

3. 빈칸에 공통으로 들어갈 말을 쓰세요.

- She __________ studying hard in the library now.
- Kevin __________ not going to wear sunglasses tomorrow.

4. 미래를 나타내는 문장이 아닌 것을 고르세요.

① We'll wait for you here.
② I'm going to take a shower tonight.
③ She is leaving for China next week.
④ Is he playing computer games now?
⑤ You won't get up early tomorrow.

5. 밑줄 친 부분을 바르게 고친 것을 고르세요.

- My family eats out last Saturday.
- Ann stayed at a hotel next weekend.

① ate – stays ② ate – is staying
③ will eat – stays ④ is eating – stays
⑤ will eat – will stay

6. 시제가 나머지와 다른 것을 고르세요.

① I learned Spanish last year.
② Did Susan know the news?
③ Joseph is helping his mom now.
④ She watered the flowers yesterday.
⑤ My brothers and I went swimming.

Words **take medicine** 약을 복용하다 **race** 경주, 달리기 (시합) **sunglasses** 선글라스 **leave for** ~로 떠나다 **Spanish** 스페인어

[7-8] 빈칸에 알맞은 말이 바르게 짝지어진 것을 고르세요.

7.

- Peter ______________ chess right now.
- Look at the clouds. It ______________ soon.

① plays – rains
② plays – will rain
③ is playing – rained
④ is playing – rains
⑤ is playing – is going to rain

8.

- David ____________ a mountain every morning.
- My sister ____________ a new bag last Tuesday.

① climbs – buys
② climbs – bought
③ is climbing – bought
④ is climbing – will buy
⑤ will climb – is buying

9. 밑줄 친 부분이 어색한 것을 고르세요.

① The bus is coming in 5 minutes.
② The test yesterday wasn't easy.
③ A little girl cried on the street right now.
④ He is going to wash the dishes soon.
⑤ They won't travel to Europe next month.

10. 질문에 대한 대답으로 알맞지 않은 것을 고르세요.

Did you watch the news last night?

① Yes, I watched it.
② No, I wasn't at home.
③ Yes, I'm watching it.
④ Of course. It was shocking.
⑤ No, I didn't. I went to bed early.

Words **play chess** 체스를 하다 **shocking** 충격적인

11. 틀린 문장을 고르세요.

① He goes on a picnic last week.

② Did she buy concert tickets?

③ I call my grandparents on Sundays.

④ My aunt is not going to sell her ring.

⑤ Jenny is walking across the road now.

[12-13] 주어진 단어를 이용하여 빈칸에 알맞은 말을 쓰세요.

서술형

12.

A: __________ the summer camp fun last year? (be)

B: Yes, it was. I __________ __________ again next year. (go)

서술형

13.

A: Many people __________ Christmas every year. (celebrate)

B: Right. My family __________ a big party last Christmas. (have)

서술형

14. 우리말과 같은 뜻이 되도록 주어진 말을 이용하여 문장을 완성하세요.

너는 어제 일을 늦게 마쳤니?

(finish your work)

→ ______________________________

late yesterday?

서술형

15. 우리말과 같은 뜻이 되도록 주어진 말을 바르게 배열하세요.

우리는 금요일에 치킨을 먹을 거야.

(on Friday / chicken / are / we / having)

→ ______________________________

____

Words **ring** 반지 **road** 도로 **summer camp** 여름 캠프

UNIT 04

can, must
may

Vocab Check! 이번 과에서 배울 단어의 뜻을 확인하고, 모르는 단어에 체크 표시하세요.

1	bring	동 가져오다	11	fly	동 날다	21	order	동 주문하다
2	return	동 반납하다	12	close	동 닫다	22	human	명 인간
3	area	명 지역, 구역	13	future	형 미래의	23	contact	동 연락하다
4	usually	부 보통	14	parrot	명 앵무새	24	password	명 암호
5	save	동 저축하다, 모으다	15	phone	동 전화하다	25	spoon	명 숟가락
6	follow	동 따르다	16	lock	동 잠그다	26	relax	동 쉬다, 휴식을 취하다
7	outside	부 밖에서	17	in danger	위험에 처한	27	magician	명 마법사
8	marathon	명 마라톤	18	lift	동 들어올리다	28	dragon	명 용
9	arrive	동 도착하다	19	heavy	형 무거운	29	medicine	명 약
10	airport	명 공항	20	station	명 역	30	get into	~에 들어가다

UNIT 04 can, must, may

I **can** swim very well.
나는 수영을 매우 잘할 수 있어요.

You **must** warm up first.
당신은 먼저 준비운동을 해야 해요.

You **may** swim here.
당신은 이곳에서 수영을 해도 좋아요.

A 조동사+동사원형

can, must, may와 같이 동사의 앞에서 동사의 의미를 보충해주는 말을 조동사라고 해요.
조동사 다음에는 항상 동사원형을 써야 해요.

주어	+	can (~할 수 있다) must (~해야 한다) may (~해도 좋다) will (~할 것이다)	+	동사원형

조동사는 주어의 인칭과 수에 상관없이 동일한 형태로 사용해요.

Jessica can goes there. (X) ⇨ Jessica **can go** there.
You must went there. (X) ⇨ You **must go** there.

canol '~할 수 있다'라는 의미로 쓰일 때만 be able to로 바꿔 쓸 수 있어요.

B can

1. 능력: ~할 수 있다

can이 '~할 수 있다'라는 능력의 뜻을 나타내며, 이때 be able to와 바꿔 쓸 수 있어요.

can	swim finish cook

I **can swim**. = I **am able to swim**.
We **can finish** the work.
= We **are able to finish** the work.
Alex **can cook** well.
= Alex **is able to cook** well.

2. 허가: ~해도 좋다

can은 '~해도 좋다'라는 허가의 뜻을 나타내기도 하는데, 이때는 may와 바꿔 쓸 수 있어요.

can	go use

You **can open** the window.
= You **may open** the window.
≠ You **are able to open** the window.

C must

must는 '~해야 한다'라는 의무의 뜻을 나타내며, have to로 바꿔 쓸 수 있어요.

must	wait be read

I **must wait** for him.
= I **have to wait** for him.
You **must be** quiet in class.
= You **have to be** quiet in class.
Monica **must read** the book.
= Monica **has to read** the book.

D may

May는 '~해도 좋다'라는 허가의 뜻을 나타내요. 이때는 can과 바꿔 쓸 수 있어요.

may	use come

May I **come** in? = **Can** I **come** in?
You **may use** my phone.
= You **can use** my phone.

My Grammar Notes

1 조동사는 동사에 의미를 더해주는 말로, 항상 ____________과 함께 쓴다.
drive (운전하다) → can drive (운전할 수 있다)
finish (끝내다) → must finish (끝내야 한다)

2 can (1) ~할 수 있다 (= be ____________ to) (2) ~해도 좋다 (= may)

3 ____________: ~해야 한다 (= have[has] to)

4 ____________: ~해도 좋다 (= can)

Warm-Up

A 조동사를 찾아 O 표시하세요. 조동사

1. You must wash the dishes.
2. She can play tennis very well.
3. You may bring your cup.
4. I will buy some clothes.
5. I must say sorry to him.
6. Mark can finish a marathon.
7. Charles will attend the meeting.
8. Suji may come to my house tonight.

Words

bring 가져오다
say sorry 사과하다
finish 끝내다
marathon 마라톤
attend 참석하다
meeting 회의
usually 보통
save 저축하다, 모으다
laptop 노트북 컴퓨터
Chinese 중국어
outside 밖에서

B ( ) 안에서 알맞은 것을 고르세요. 조동사+동사원형

1. 1) Martin must (go / goes) home now.
   2) Martin usually (go / goes) home at six.
2. 1) I must (save / saves) money.
   2) I won't (buy / buys) a new laptop.
3. 1) Yuna (speak / speaks) English very well.
   2) Yuna can (speak / speaks) Chinese, too.
4. 1) David (finish / finished) his homework.
   2) David may (play / plays) outside.
5. 1) Amy (like / likes) cooking.
   2) Amy will (make / makes) pizza for me.

C 밑줄 친 부분의 의미로 알맞은 것을 고르세요. 조동사의 의미

1. You must listen to me. (~할 수 있다 / ~해야 한다)
2. Tina is able to play the flute. (~할 수 있다 / ~해도 좋다)
3. You may swim in this river. (~해야 한다 / ~해도 좋다)
4. We must follow safety rules. (~해야 한다 / ~해도 좋다)
5. He has to wear a school uniform. (~할 수 있다 / ~해야 한다)
6. We can win the soccer game. (~할 수 있다 / ~해도 좋다)
7. You may buy a new camera. (~해야 한다 / ~해도 좋다)
8. They can pass the exam. (~할 수 있다 / ~해야 한다)

Words

flute (악기) 플루트
follow 따르다
safety 안전
rule 규칙
school uniform 교복
win 이기다
exam 시험
arrive 도착하다
airport 공항

D 두 문장이 같은 의미가 되도록 ( ) 안에서 알맞은 것을 고르세요.

조동사의 의미

1. I can ride a horse.
   = I (am able to / have to) ride a horse.
2. She must wait for the bus.
   = She (is able to / has to) wait for the bus.
3. Frank can drive a car.
   = Frank (is able to / has to) drive a car.
4. You must arrive at the airport by 12.
   = You (are able to / have to) arrive at the airport by 12.
5. You can have more ice cream.
   = You (are able to / may) have more ice cream.

Practice

A 밑줄 친 부분에 해당하는 의미를 보기에서 고르세요.

보기 ⓐ ~할 수 있다 ⓑ ~해도 좋다 ⓒ ~해야 한다

1. Juno <u>can</u> run very fast. ⓐ
2. You <u>may</u> have this cake.
3. The parrot <u>is able to</u> speak.
4. You <u>have to</u> take a blood test.
5. The children <u>must</u> buy tickets.
6. Is he ill? He <u>can</u> go home now.
7. You <u>may</u> take pictures in this area.
8. Peter Pan and Tinkerbell <u>are able to</u> fly.
9. My brother <u>can</u> sing many pop songs.
10. You <u>may</u> use my computer for an hour.
11. Are you cold? You <u>can</u> close the window.
12. You <u>have to</u> take a shower after exercising.
13. She <u>must</u> take this medicine once a day.
14. Mina <u>has to</u> cook for her mom's birthday party.
15. Elephants <u>can</u> carry heavy things with their trunks.

Words

parrot 앵무새
blood test 혈액 검사
ticket 표, 티켓
ill 아픈
area 지역, 구역
fly 날다
pop song 대중가요, 팝송
use 사용하다
for an hour 한 시간 동안
close 닫다
take a shower 샤워하다
medicine 약
once a day 하루에 한 번
carry (짐을) 나르다
heavy 무거운
trunk (코끼리의) 코

B 두 문장이 같은 의미가 되도록 빈칸에 알맞은 말을 쓰세요.

1. My brother can read French.
   = My brother is able to read French.
2. She must phone home right now.
   = She ______ ______ phone home right now.
3. You may have a hamburger and Coke.
   = You ______ have a hamburger and Coke.
4. I have to return the books today.
   = I ______ return the books today.
5. We can move the box.
   = We ______ ______ ______ move the box.
6. You can get into the concert hall now.
   = You ______ get into the concert hall now.

Words

French 프랑스어
phone 전화하다
right now 지금 당장
return 반납하다
move 옮기다
get into ~에 들어가다
concert hall 콘서트 홀
jump (제자리에서) 뛰다
high 높이
cello 첼로
count (수를) 세다
driver 운전자
follow 따르다
traffic 교통

C 밑줄 친 부분을 바르게 고쳐 쓰세요.

1. I be able to jump high. → am able to
2. She able to play the cello. → ______
3. Tim may visits me on Friday. → ______
4. You must have to save money. → ______
5. He have to buy a ticket for the train. → ______
6. The child cans count to ten in English. → ______
7. Drivers must followed the traffic rules. → ______

D 두 문장의 의미가 같으면 O, 그렇지 않으면 X 표시하세요.

1. 1) You can join us.
   2) You may join us. O

2. 1) He can begin the work today.
   2) He has to begin the work today.

3. 1) I can walk to school.
   2) I'm able to walk to school.

4. 1) You must remember the password.
   2) You have to remember the password.

5. 1) They must check out these books.
   2) They are able to check out these books.

Words

join 함께 하다
password 암호
check out (책을) 빌리다, 대출하다
lift 들어올리다
stone 돌
station 역
chameleon 카멜레온
change 바꾸다
skin 피부
lock 잠그다
garage 차고

E 우리말을 영어로 바르게 표현한 것을 고르세요.

1. 그는 그 무거운 돌을 들 수 있다.
   ① He may lift the heavy stone.
   ② He can lift the heavy stone.

2. 그녀는 8시까지 기차역에 가야 한다.
   ① She can go to the train station by 8.
   ② She must go to the train station by 8.

3. 카멜레온은 피부 색깔을 바꿀 수 있다.
   ① Chameleons have to change their skin color.
   ② Chameleons are able to change their skin color.

4. 너는 지금 차고 문을 잠가도 돼.
   ① You may lock the garage door now.
   ② You must lock the garage door now.

F 우리말과 같은 뜻이 되도록 can, may, must를 이용하여 문장을 완성하세요.

1. 그는 영어로 일기를 쓸 수 있다. (write)
→ He can write his diary in English.

2. 그녀는 다음 주까지 여기에 머물러야 한다. (stay)
→ She ______ here until next week.

3. 내 코트를 입어도 좋아. (wear)
→ You ______ my coat.

4. 나는 중국어와 프랑스어를 말할 수 있다. (speak)
→ I ______ Chinese and French.

5. 너는 매일 바이올린을 연습해야 한다. (practice)
→ You ______ the violin every day.

6. 우리는 그 일을 내일까지 끝낼 수 있다. (finish)
→ We ______ the work by tomorrow.

7. 저 우산 중에서 하나를 가져도 괜찮아. (have)
→ You ______ one of those umbrellas.

8. 우리는 이메일로 서로 연락할 수 있다. (contact)
→ We ______ each other by e-mail.

9. 그는 이번 달에 출장을 가야만 한다. (go)
→ He ______ on a business trip this month.

10. 그 마법사는 저 고양이를 용으로 바꿀 수 있다. (change)
→ The magician ______ the cat into a dragon.

Words

diary 일기(장)
until ~까지
work 일하다; 일
contact 연락하다
each other 서로
go on a business trip 출장을 가다
magician 마법사
dragon 용

Grammar into Writing

A 우리말과 같은 뜻이 되도록 주어진 말을 바르게 배열하세요.

1. 너는 네 방을 청소해야 한다. your room / must / you / clean

→ You must clean your room.

2. Joe는 파스타를 만들 수 있다. is / make / pasta / able / Joe / to

→ ______

3. 그는 그 문을 고쳐야 한다. to / fix / he / the door / has

→ ______

4. 그녀는 트럭을 운전할 수 있다. a truck / she / can / drive

→ ______

5. 너희들은 지금 떠나도 좋다. you / leave / can / now

→ ______

6. 그들은 7시 전에 쇼를 시작해야 한다. must / they / before 7 / start / the show

→ ______

B 우리말과 같은 뜻이 되도록 be able to 또는 have to를 이용하여 문장을 만드세요.

1. Cindy는 케이크를 구울 수 있다. (bake cakes)

→ Cindy is able to bake cakes.

2. 그는 내일 일찍 일어나야 한다. (get up early, tomorrow)

→ ______

3. 나는 영어로 이야기를 쓸 수 있다. (write stories, in English)

→ ______________________________

4. 그녀는 스케이트를 매우 잘 탈 수 있다. (skate, very well)

→ ______________________________

5. 당신은 줄을 서서 기다려야 합니다. (wait in line)

→ ______________________________

6. 나는 여동생을 위해 선물을 사야 한다. (buy a gift, for my sister)

→ ______________________________

7. 우리는 스마트폰으로 영화를 만들 수 있다. (make films, with smartphones)

→ ______________________________

C 다음 글을 읽고 틀린 부분을 찾아 표시한 다음, 고쳐서 다시 써보세요.

This is Future Town. There are many robots here. The robots look like humans. They can be able to think and act like humans. They must helps people in danger. Some robots can even flying and saving people. These robots are really cool!

↓

This is Future Town. ______________________________

____

____

Words

wait in line 줄 서서 기다리다 **film** 영화 **future** 미래의 **robot** 로봇 **look like** ~처럼 보이다 **human** 인간 **act** 행동하다 **in danger** 위험에 처한 **even** 심지어 **cool** 멋진

Wrap-Up Test

1. 밑줄 친 말과 바꿔 쓸 수 있는 것을 고르세요.

> I have an essay in German. I am able to read it.

① may ② can ③ must
④ have to ⑤ will

2. 빈칸에 알맞은 말을 고르세요.

> A: Excuse me, this computer doesn't work.
> B: Oh, you ______________ enter the password first.

① must ② can ③ will
④ may ⑤ are able to

3. 밑줄 친 부분의 의미가 바르지 않은 것을 고르세요.

① You must go to school now. – 가야 한다
② I'm able to play the piano. – 연주할 수 있다
③ He can sing well. – 노래할 수 있다
④ He has to finish the work. – 끝내야 한다
⑤ You may wear my jacket. – 입어야 한다

[4-5] 우리말을 영어로 바르게 옮긴 것을 고르세요.

4.

> 난 지금 너를 집에 데려다줄 수 있어.

① I will take you home now.
② I can take you home now.
③ You may take me home now.
④ You must take me home now.
⑤ I have to take you home now.

5.

> 그는 버스를 운전해야 한다.

① He will drive a bus.
② He can drive a bus.
③ He may drive a bus.
④ He must drive a bus.
⑤ He is able to drive a bus.

Words **essay** 수필 **work** 일; 작동하다 **German** 독일어 **enter** 입력하다 **take ~ home** ~를 집에 데려다주다

6. 빈칸에 알맞은 말이 바르게 짝지어진 것을 고르세요.

• You have to ________ the English test.

• She can ________ 100 meters in 15 seconds.

① take – run ② took – ran

③ took – run ④ take – runs

⑤ taking – runs

7. can이 보기와 같은 의미로 쓰인 것을 고르세요.

보기 Robert can speak Korean.

① He can stay here.

② She can use my spoon.

③ I can pass the math exam.

④ You can come to the party.

⑤ You can go shopping with me.

8. 빈칸에 들어갈 수 없는 것을 고르세요.

A: I feel sick now.

B: Really? ________________

① You must see a doctor.

② You have to relax now.

③ I can call a doctor for you.

④ You must take some medicine.

⑤ You're able to go to the hospital.

9. 밑줄 친 부분을 may로 바꿔 쓸 수 없는 것을 고르세요.

① A: I'm tired today.
B: You can go home now.

② A: I can swim well.
B: Then let's go swimming.

③ A: I'll wait for you outside.
B: You can come in my room.

④ A: It's cold in here.
B: You can close the window.

⑤ A: I want to eat Jack's cookies.
B: You can eat some.

Words
take a test 시험 보다 **meter** (거리) 미터 **second** (시간) 초 **spoon** 숟가락
relax 쉬다, 휴식을 취하다 **hospital** 병원

10. 틀린 문장을 고르세요.

① I must go to school by 7.

② Jina is able to drive a car.

③ You can go out after dinner.

④ She can solved the problem.

⑤ Alex must study for the quiz.

11. 밑줄 친 부분이 바르게 쓰인 것을 고르세요.

① She must visit her uncle.

② We is able to sing the song.

③ He may wants a new bicycle.

④ She has to is ready for the exam.

⑤ You may ordering some ice cream.

서술형

12. 빈칸에 알맞은 말을 써서 대화를 완성하세요.

A: Sally, let's go to the park after school.
B: Sorry, I can't. I __________ __________ go to my yoga class.

서술형

13. 우리말과 같은 뜻이 되도록 주어진 말을 이용하여 문장을 완성하세요.

The children __________ __________ __________ __________ bikes. (ride)
(그 아이들은 자전거를 탈 수 있다.)

서술형

14. 우리말과 같은 뜻이 되도록 주어진 말을 바르게 배열하세요.

돈이 있으니, 너는 이 가방을 사도 좋다.
(buy / this / bag / may)

→ You have money, so you __________ __________ __________ __________.

서술형

15. 틀린 부분을 찾아 바르게 고쳐 쓰세요.

Molly have to leave right now.
(Molly는 지금 당장 떠나야 한다.)

__________ → __________

Words **solve** 풀다, 해결하다 **quiz** 퀴즈, 쪽지시험 **be ready for** ~에 준비가 되다 **order** 주문하다 **yoga** 요가

UNIT 05

조동사의 부정문

Vocab Check! 이번 과에서 배울 단어의 뜻을 확인하고, 모르는 단어에 체크 표시하세요.

1	noisy	형 시끄러운	11	alone	부 혼자	21	quickly	부 빠르게
2	textbook	명 교과서	12	park	동 주차하다 명 공원	22	borrow	동 빌리다
3	give up	포기하다	13	touch	동 만지다	23	health	명 건강
4	chance	명 기회	14	wild	형 사나운	24	secret	명 비밀
5	understand	동 이해하다	15	enter	동 들어가다	25	rule	명 규칙
6	trash	명 쓰레기	16	worry	동 걱정하다	26	barefoot	부 맨발로
7	difficult	형 어려운	17	regularly	부 규칙적으로	27	answer	동 대답하다
8	deep	형 깊은	18	hurry	동 서두르다	28	spicy	형 자극적인, 매운
9	waste	동 낭비하다	19	riddle	명 수수께끼	29	carrot	명 당근
10	grass	명 풀밭	20	passport	명 여권	30	adult	명 어른

UNIT 05 조동사의 부정문

You must not use your phone.
당신은 전화를 사용해서는 안 돼요.

You may not make noise.
당신은 큰 소리를 내서는 안 돼요.

You cannot take pictures of the movie.
당신은 영화 사진을 찍어서는 안 돼요.

A 조동사의 부정문: 조동사+not+동사원형

조동사의 부정문은 조동사 뒤에 not을 써서 만들 수 있어요.

주어	+	**cannot** (~할 수 없다) **must not** (~해서는 안 된다) **may not** (~해서는 안 된다)	+	동사원형

B cannot (= can't)

can의 부정문은 cannot으로 쓰고, can't로 줄여 쓸 수도 있어요.

불가능을 뜻하는 cannot은 be not able to와 바꿔 쓸 수 있어요.

1. 불가능: ~할 수 없다

능력·가능의 can 뒤에 not을 붙이면 '~할 수 없다'라는 뜻으로 불가능을 나타내요.

cannot	do swim play

He **cannot swim** well.
= He **is not able to swim** well.
We **can't play** tennis.
= We **aren't able to play** tennis.

2. 금지: ~해서는 안 된다

허가의 can 뒤에 not을 붙이면 '~해서는 안 된다'의 뜻으로 금지를 나타내요.
이때 may not과 바꿔 쓸 수 있어요.

'금지'를 나타내는 cannot 대신 be not able to는 쓸 수 없어요.

cannot	go eat open

You **can't go** out tonight.
= You **may not go** out tonight.
The box is hers. You **cannot open** it.
≠ You **are not able to open** it.

C must not와 don't have to

'~해야 한다'라는 의무의 뜻을 가진 must는 have to와 바꾸어 쓸 수 있지만, must의 부정은 have to의 부정과 뜻이 다르므로 주의해야 해요.

1. must not (= mustn't): ~해서는 안 된다

의무의 must 뒤에 not을 붙이면 '~해서는 안 된다'라는 강한 금지를 나타내요.

must not	play tell

You **must not play** outside.
= You **mustn't play** outside.
We **mustn't tell** a lie.

must not은 cannot이나 may not보다 훨씬 강한 금지를 나타내요.

2. don't have to: ~할 필요가 없다

의무의 have to 앞에 don't를 붙이면 '~할 필요가 없다'는 부정의 의미를 나타내요.

don't have to	bring call

You **don't have to bring** a lunchbox.
He **doesn't have to call** me.

D may not

허가의 may 뒤에 not을 붙이면 '~해서는 안 된다'라는 금지를 나타내요.
이때 cannot(= can't)과 바꿔 쓸 수 있어요.

must not	park

You **may not park** here.
= You **cannot park** here.

My Grammar Notes

1 조동사의 부정문: 주어+조동사+ ____________ + ____________ ~
I ____________ play the violin. (나는 바이올린을 연주하지 못한다.)
You must ____________ walk on the grass. (잔디를 밟아서는 안 된다.)

2 cannot(= can't) (1) ~할 수 없다 (2) ~해서는 안 된다 (= ____________ not)

3 must not: ~해서는 안 된다 (강한 금지)
don't[doesn't] ____________ ____________: ~할 필요가 없다

Warm-Up

A 표지판의 의미를 바르게 나타낸 것을 고르세요. 조동사의 부정문

1. 
① You can smoke here.
② You cannot smoke here.

2. 
① You must swim here.
② You must not swim here.

3. 
① You can't take pictures here.
② You can take pictures here.

4. 
① You may bring your dog here.
② You may not bring your dog here.

5. 
① You must ride a bike here.
② You must not ride a bike here.

Words

smoke 담배를 피우다
swim 수영하다
bring 가져오다, 데려오다
fast food 패스트푸드
movie ticket 영화표
outside 밖에
at night 밤에
during ~ 동안

B ( ) 안에서 알맞은 것을 고르세요. 조동사의 부정문

1. Mira (can't finish / can't finishes) her work.
2. They (aren't able to / are able not to) speak Chinese.
3. He (must not eat / must eat not) fast food.
4. Keira (don't have to / doesn't have to) buy movie tickets.
5. You (may not go / may go not) outside at night.
6. You (can't wear / can't wore) a hat during the test.

C 밑줄 친 부분을 부정형으로 바꿔 쓰세요. 조동사의 부정문

1. I can open the door. → can't
2. We must eat food now. →
3. You have to run fast. →
4. You may get up late. →
5. Dan has to work hard. →
6. Claire is able to ride a horse. →

Words

hard 열심히
horse 말
join 참가하다; 가입하다
return 돌려주다; 반납하다
climb 등반하다
mountain 산
give up 포기하다
chance 기회

D 우리말과 같은 뜻이 되도록 ( ) 안에서 알맞은 것을 고르세요.

조동사의 부정문

1. 나는 그 경기에 참가할 수 없다.
   → I (can / can't) join the game.
2. 너희들은 그 TV 프로그램을 보면 안 된다.
   → You (may / may not) watch the TV program.
3. 너는 그 책을 오늘 반납할 필요가 없다.
   → You (have to / don't have to) return the book today.
4. Bella는 9시에 잠자리에 들어야 한다.
   → Bella (must / must not) go to bed at 9.
5. 그는 그 산을 올라갈 수 있다.
   → He (can / can't) climb the mountain.
6. 너는 그 기회를 포기하면 안 된다.
   → You (must / must not) give up the chance.

Practice

A 밑줄 친 부분이 be not able to와 같은 의미이면 바꿔 쓰고, 다른 의미이면 X 표시하세요.

1. I can't understand you. → am not able to
2. She cannot speak English. →
3. You can't eat food in the museum. →
4. It's too late. You cannot go out. →
5. They can't finish a marathon. →
6. I can't solve the problem. It's difficult. →
7. He can't buy the car. He doesn't have money.

   →

Words

understand 이해하다
museum 박물관
solve (문제를) 풀다
difficult 어려운
waste 낭비하다
pay 지불하다
free 무료의
hospital 병원
grass 풀밭
touch 만지다
wild 사나운
noisy 시끄러운
camp 야영하다
safe 안전한

B ( ) 안에서 알맞은 것을 고르세요.

1. You (must not / don't have to) waste your time. Time is money.
2. You (must not / don't have to) pay for the ticket. It's free.
3. I (must not / don't have to) go to the hospital. I feel okay.
4. You (mustn't / don't have to) walk on the grass.
5. You (must not / don't have to) touch the dog. It's wild.
6. She (must not / doesn't have to) get up early on Sundays.
7. We (mustn't / don't have to) play the cello at night. It's noisy.

C 밑줄 친 부분의 의미가 같으면 O, 그렇지 않으면 X 표시하세요.

1. 1) You <u>can't</u> talk with friends in the library. O
   2) You <u>may not</u> enter the room.

2. 1) You <u>can</u> play soccer well.
   2) She <u>is able to</u> read books quickly.

3. 1) He <u>doesn't have to</u> work tomorrow.
   2) You <u>don't have to</u> worry about me.

4. 1) You <u>may not</u> bring outside food.
   2) I <u>cannot</u> remember his name.

5. 1) You <u>must not</u> drive so fast.
   2) We <u>don't have to</u> hurry.

6. 1) All teachers <u>have to</u> teach first aid to students.
   2) Students <u>must</u> practice it once a month.

D 밑줄 친 부분을 바르게 고쳐 쓰세요.

1. She <u>don't have to</u> stay here. → doesn't have to
2. You <u>must do not</u> make noise. →
3. She cannot <u>dances</u> well. →
4. You <u>may bring not</u> textbooks. →
5. John and I <u>isn't able to</u> swim well. →
6. I <u>can't not go</u> to the concert today. →

Words

library 도서관
enter 들어가다
quickly 빠르게
worry 걱정하다
hurry 서두르다
first aid 응급 처치
stay 머무르다
make noise 시끄럽게 하다
textbook 교과서

E ( ) 안에서 알맞은 것을 고르세요.

1. I (can / can't) go to the movies. I feel sick.
2. I (can / can't) open the door. I lost the key.
3. Terry (is / isn't) able to pass the exam. He's smart.
4. I'm sorry. I (can / can't) join your birthday party.
5. You (may / may not) borrow my book. I finished it.
6. You (may / may not) leave now. You finished the work.
7. You (must / mustn't) change your password regularly.
8. You (may / may not) play music. The baby is sleeping.
9. You (have to / don't have to) clean your room. It's dirty.
10. We (must / don't have to) be quiet. People are studying.
11. She (can / can't) drive well. She is a good driver.
12. You (have to / don't have to) wear a coat. It's very cold outside.
13. He (is / isn't) able to travel to England. He doesn't have a passport.
14. You (must / mustn't) sit on the chair. I painted it a few minutes ago.
15. Emily (has to / doesn't have to) worry about me. I can do it myself.

Words

sick 아픈
lose 잃어버리다 (과거형 **lost**)
pass 통과하다, 합격하다
smart 똑똑한
borrow 빌리다
leave 떠나다; 남겨 두다
password 비밀번호
regularly 규칙적으로
dirty 더러운
quiet 조용한
passport 여권
paint 페인트 칠하다
a few minutes ago 몇 분 전에
do it oneself 혼자서 하다

F 우리말과 같은 뜻이 되도록 보기와 주어진 단어를 이용하여 문장을 완성하세요. 필요하면 형태를 바꾸세요.

보기 must can have to may be able to

1. 이 강에서 수영을 해서는 안 된다. (swim)
→ You must not swim in this river.

2. 우리는 약속을 지켜야 한다. (keep)
→ We ______ ______ our promises.

3. 나는 여기서 내 친구를 찾을 수가 없다. (find)
→ I ______ ______ my friend here.

4. 그는 비밀을 말하면 안 된다. (tell)
→ He ______ ______ the secret.

5. 나는 오늘 출근할 필요가 없다. (go)
→ I ______ ______ ______ ______ to work today.

6. Robert는 일본어를 할 수 있다. (speak)
→ Robert ______ ______ ______ speak Japanese.

7. 그녀는 그 회의에 참석하지 않아도 된다. (attend)
→ She ______ ______ ______ ______ the meeting.

8. 그들은 그 무거운 상자를 옮기지 못한다. (carry)
→ They ______ ______ ______ ______ carry the heavy box.

9. 그녀는 건강을 위해 아침 식사를 해야 한다. (have)
→ She ______ ______ ______ breakfast for her health.

Words

keep one's promise 약속을 지키다
secret 비밀
attend 참석하다
meeting 회의
carry 옮기다, 나르다
heavy 무거운
health 건강

Grammar into Writing

A 우리말과 같은 뜻이 되도록 보기와 주어진 말을 이용하여 문장을 만드세요.

보기		
come early	travel alone	go to school tomorrow
drive a car	solve the riddle	smoke in this building

1. 그녀는 혼자 여행해서는 안 된다. (must)
   → She must not travel alone.
2. 우리는 내일 학교에 갈 필요가 없다. (have to)
   → ______________________
3. 나는 운전을 하지 못한다. (can)
   → ______________________
4. 이 건물에서 담배를 피워서는 안 됩니다. (may)
   → ______________________
5. 그녀는 일찍 올 필요가 없다. (have to)
   → ______________________
6. 우리는 그 수수께끼를 풀 수 없다. (be able to)
   → ______________________

B 우리말과 같은 뜻이 되도록 바르게 고쳐 쓰세요.

1. I may not find my watch. (나는 내 시계를 찾을 수가 없다.)
   → I cannot find my watch.
2. You must pick the flowers. (그 꽃을 꺾어서는 안 된다.)
   → ______________________

3. He must not work today. (그는 오늘 일할 필요가 없다.)

→ ______________________________

4. You can bring your dog inside. (개를 안으로 데려올 수 없어요.)

→ ______________________________

5. You may not meet Alice today. (너는 오늘 Alice를 만날 필요가 없다.)

→ ______________________________

6. The baby birds are able to fly. (아기 새들은 날지 못한다.)

→ ______________________________

C 다음 글을 읽고, 밑줄 친 부분을 바르게 고쳐 쓰세요.

Welcome to the Taj Mahal! You ❶ can know about some rules. First, you ❷ may wear short clothes. Short clothes are rude in this place. Second, you ❸ don't have to put on your socks. You cannot walk barefoot. And you ❹ must take photos inside. But you can do it outside. Enjoy your tour!

↓

❶ must know ❷ ______________

❸ ______________ ❹ ______________

Words **alone** 혼자 **riddle** 수수께끼 **pick** 고르다; 꺾다 **Taj Mahal** 타지마할(인도에 있는 궁전 형식의 묘지) **rule** 규칙 **rude** 무례한 **put on** (옷을) 입다 **barefoot** 맨발의, 맨발로 **tour** 여행, 관광

Wrap-Up Test

[1-2] 빈칸에 알맞은 말을 고르세요.

1.

A: I __________ lift this box. It's heavy.

B: I can help you.

① can ② cannot ③ may

④ may not ⑤ am able to

2.

A: Excuse me. You __________ park here.

B: Why not?

A: This place is for disabled people. Park over there.

① can ② may ③ must

④ must not ⑤ don't have to

3. 빈칸에 들어갈 수 없는 것을 고르세요.

Young children ____________ swim in the river. It's too deep.

① can't ② cannot ③ mustn't

④ may not ⑤ don't have to

4. 밑줄 친 부분과 같은 의미로 쓰인 것을 고르세요.

My son isn't able to write his name.

① cannot ② will not

③ may not ④ must not

⑤ doesn't have to

5. 빈칸에 알맞은 말이 바르게 짝지어진 것을 고르세요.

- I don't have a key. So I __________ open the door.
- Pick up your trash. You __________ leave it in the park.

① may not – can

② can – may not

③ cannot – must not

④ may – don't have to

⑤ don't have to – may

Words **lift** 들어올리다 **park** 주차하다; 공원 **disabled people** 장애인 **deep** 깊은 **pick up** 줍다, 집어올리다 **trash** 쓰레기

6. 우리말을 영어로 바르게 옮긴 것을 고르세요.

그녀는 다이어트를 할 필요가 없다.

① She cannot go on a diet.
② She may not go on a diet.
③ She must not go on a diet.
④ She is not able to go on a diet.
⑤ She doesn't have to go on a diet.

7. 밑줄 친 부분이 올바른 것을 고르세요.

① You not be able to sit here.
② We must not leave him alone.
③ Mom cannot washes the dishes.
④ He don't have to borrow a camera.
⑤ She not may walk down the street.

8. 빈칸에 not이 들어갈 수 없는 것을 고르세요.

① She may _________ join our club.
② You must _________ open the door.
③ We have to _________ take the taxi.
④ They are _________ able to help you.
⑤ I will _________ cook potato soup.

9. 우리말과 영어가 잘못 짝지어진 것을 고르세요.

① 그녀는 당근을 사야 합니다.
→ She has to buy carrots.
② 그는 프랑스어를 말할 줄 모릅니다.
→ He cannot speak French.
③ 저는 버스를 탈 필요가 없습니다.
→ I don't have to ride a bus.
④ 우리는 그녀를 깨워서는 안 됩니다.
→ We may not wake her up.
⑤ 당신은 창문을 열어서는 안 됩니다.
→ You are not able to open the window.

10. 틀린 문장을 고르세요.

① You may not stay here.
② David can't eat spicy food.
③ He doesn't have to go to school.
④ She must use not my laptop.
⑤ I am not able to check my e-mail.

Words **go on a diet** 다이어트를 하다 **carrot** 당근 **spicy** 자극적인, 매운 **check** 확인하다

[11-12] 두 문장이 같은 의미가 되도록 빈칸에 알맞은 말을 쓰세요.

서술형

11.

He cannot take good pictures well.

= He ________ ________ ________ ________ take good pictures well.

서술형

12.

You must be quiet in the library.

= You ________ ________ make noise in the library.

서술형

13. **우리말과 같은 뜻이 되도록 틀린 부분을 찾아 바르게 고쳐 쓰세요.**

She may not answer the question.
(그녀는 그 질문에 대답할 필요가 없습니다.)

________ → ________

[14-15] 안내문을 읽고, 물음에 답하세요.

Welcome to the Central Museum!

- Opening hours: 9 a.m. – 5 p.m.
- Admission fee: Adults ($10), Children ($5)
- (cannot / drinks / you / bring)

※ The museum is closed on Mondays.

서술형

14. **우리말과 같은 뜻이 되도록 ( ) 안의 단어를 바르게 배열하세요.**

당신은 음료를 가지고 와서는 안 됩니다.

→ ________________

15. **윗글의 내용과 일치하도록 ( ) 안에서 알맞은 것을 고르세요.**

(1) You (have to / don't have to) pay to enter the museum.

(2) You (can / can't) get into the museum on Mondays.

(3) You (are / aren't) able to enter the museum at six.

Words **answer** 대답하다 **central museum** 중앙 박물관 **opening hours** 개장 시간 **admission fee** 입장료 **adult** 어른 **get into** ~에 들어가다

UNIT 06

조동사의 의문문

Vocab Check! 이번 과에서 배울 단어의 뜻을 확인하고, 모르는 단어에 체크 표시하세요.

No.	Word	Meaning
1	visit	동 방문하다
2	map	명 지도
3	pack	동 (짐을) 싸다
4	welcome	동 환영하다
5	bathroom	명 화장실
6	alphabet	명 알파벳
7	swimsuit	명 수영복
8	kick	동 (발로) 차다
9	during	전 ~동안
10	police	명 경찰
11	invite	동 초대하다
12	whistle	동 휘파람을 불다
13	early	부 일찍
14	sneakers	명 운동화
15	loudly	부 크게
16	try on	(옷을) 입어보다
17	register	동 등록하다
18	come back	돌아오다
19	prepare	동 준비하다
20	young	형 어린
21	face	명 얼굴
22	fine	형 좋은 명 벌금
23	helmet	명 헬멧
24	turn on	(전원을) 켜다
25	hand in	제출하다
26	fix	동 수리하다
27	reason	명 이유
28	report	명 보고서
29	exhibition	명 전시회
30	seat belt	명 안전벨트

UNIT 06 조동사의 의문문

Can you make coffee? – **Yes, I can.**
당신은 커피를 만들 수 있나요? 네, 할 수 있어요.

May I order coffee? – **Sure, you can.**
제가 커피를 주문해도 될까요? 물론이죠.

Must I give a tip to you? – **No, you don't have to.**
제가 당신에게 팁을 줘야 하나요? 아니요, 그럴 필요 없어요.

A 조동사의 의문문 만들기

조동사의 의문문은 주어와 조동사의 위치를 서로 바꾸어 만들어요.

I	**can**	go home now.	나는 지금 집에 갈 수 있어요.
Can	I	go home now**?**	지금 집에 가도 될까요?

B Can+주어 ~? / May+주어 ~?

can과 may의 의문문은 의미에 따라 다음과 같이 사용해요.

	질문		대답
능력, 가능	**Can** you **Are** you **able to** (~할 수 있나요?)	**play** the piano? (피아노를 연주할)	**Yes**, I **can**. / **Yes**, I **am**. (네, 할 수 있어요.) **No**, I **can't**. / **No**, I**'m not**. (아니요, 하지 못해요.)
요청	**Can** you (~해 줄래요?)	**go** with me? (나와 함께 가)	Sure, I **can**. / Okay. / Of course. (좋아요. / 물론이죠. / 그럼요.) Sorry, I **can't**. (죄송하지만, 안 돼요.)
허가, 허락	**Can** I **May** I (~해도 될까요?)	**open** the window? (창문을 열어도)	**Yes**, you **can[may]**. / Sure. (네, 그래도 돼요. / 그럼요.) Sorry, you **can't[may not]**. (죄송하지만, 안 돼요.)

Can she snowboard? (능력, 가능) – **Yes**, she **can**.
= **Is** she **able to** snowboard? – **No**, she **isn't**.

Can you sing a song for me? (요청) – Of course. / Sorry, I **can't**.

Can I go out and play? (허가, 허락) – Sure, you **can**.
= **May** I go out and play? – **No**, you **may not**.

C Must+주어 ~? / Do[Does]+주어+have to ~?

질문			대답
Must I **Do I have to** (내가 ~해야 하나요?)	**clean** the room? (방을 청소해야)	→	**Yes**, you **must**. (네, 그래야 해요.) **No**, you **don't have to**. (아니요, 그럴 필요 없어요.)

Must Billy take the test? (의무) – **Yes**, he **must**.
= **Does** Billy **have to** take the test? – **No**, he **doesn't have to**.

Mini Grammar

정중하게 요청하기

'~해 주시겠어요?'라고 무언가를 요청하는 경우 can 말고도 Will you ~?, Would you ~?, Could you ~?로도 표현할 수 있어요. Would[Could] you ~?가 더 정중한 표현이에요.

Would you **open** the door? (문 좀 열어주시겠어요?)

Could you **give** me a tissue, please? (휴지 좀 주시겠어요?)

My Grammar Notes

1 조동사의 의문문: __________ + __________ +동사원형 ~?

2 능력, 가능: Can you swim? = __________ you __________ __________ swim?

3 요청: __________ you take a picture of me?

4 허가, 허락: Can I use your phone? = __________ I __________ your phone?

5 의무: Must I read the book?
= Do __________ __________ __________ read the book?

Warm-Up

A 보기에서 알맞은 말을 골라 의문문을 완성하세요. 조동사의 의문문

보기 Do I May I Must I Is she Can you

1. Can you give me the book? – Sure, I can.
2. ______ wait for him? – No, you don't have to.
3. ______ go home now? – Yes, you may.
4. ______ able to play the guitar? – No, she isn't.
5. ______ have to pay now? – Yes, you do.
6. ______ read the English alphabet? – No, I can't.

Words

wait for ~를 기다리다
pay 지불하다
alphabet 알파벳
follow 따라가다
bathroom 화장실
learn 배우다
math 수학
visit 방문하다

B ( ) 안에서 알맞은 것을 고르세요. 조동사의 의문문

1. Must I (follow / following) with him?
2. Can she (speaks / speak) Korean?
3. May (use I / I use) the bathroom?
4. Are you (can / able to) get up early?
5. Must (learn I / I learn) math?
6. (Can I / Do I can) go shopping with you?
7. (Do I have to / Must I have to) visit you today?
8. (Is able your dad to / Is your dad able to) cook well?

C 우리말과 같은 뜻이 되도록 ( ) 안에서 알맞은 것을 고르세요.

조동사의 의문문

1. 제가 경찰에 연락해야 하나요?

→ (May / Must) I call the police?

2. 저를 집에 데려다 주시겠어요?

→ (Could / Must) you take me home?

3. 이 치마를 입어 봐도 될까요?

→ (May / Must) I try on this skirt?

4. 제가 오늘 이 차를 수리해야 하나요?

→ (Can / Must) I fix this car today?

5. Jerry를 파티에 초대해도 될까요?

→ (Can / Must) I invite Jerry to the party?

6. 제가 교복을 입어야 하나요?

→ (Can / Must) I wear the school uniform?

Words

police 경찰
try on (옷을) 입어보다
fix 수리하다
invite 초대하다
school uniform 교복
go for a walk 산책 가다
turn off (전원을) 끄다
skate 스케이트를 타다

D 질문에 알맞은 대답을 연결하세요.

조동사의 의문문

1. Can I join your club? •	• ⓐ Yes, you may.
2. May I go for a walk? •	• ⓑ Yes, we are.
3. Can you wait a minute? •	• ⓒ No, you don't have to.
4. Must I turn off the radio? •	• ⓓ Sorry, but you can't.
5. Are you able to skate? •	• ⓔ Yes, I do.
6. Do you have to leave now? •	• ⓕ Sure, I can.

Practice

A 우리말과 같은 뜻이 되도록 알맞은 조동사를 모두 고르세요.

1. 제가 그 책을 읽어도 돼요? (Can / May / Must) I read the book?
2. 피아노를 칠 수 있나요? (Can / May / Must) you play the piano?
3. 정원을 구경해도 돼요? (Can / May / Must) I see your garden?
4. 나에게 5달러를 빌려줄래요? (Can / May / Must) you lend me $5?
5. 그는 오늘 돌아와야 하나요?
   (Can / May / Must) he come back today?
6. 제가 이 일을 지금 당장 끝내야 하나요?
   (Can / May / Must) I finish this work right now?
7. Michelle은 체스를 둘 수 있나요?
   (Can / May / Must) Michelle play chess?

Words

lend 빌려주다
come back 돌아오다
chess 체스
solve 풀다, 해결하다
problem 문제
anytime 언제든지
for a minute 잠시 동안
health 건강
pack (짐을) 싸다

B 밑줄 친 부분의 의미가 같으면 O, 그렇지 않으면 X 표시하세요.

1. 1) You look bad. You may go home now. X
   2) Can you solve the problem?
2. 1) You can visit us anytime.
   2) May I talk to you for a minute?
3. 1) Can I have some more cookies?
   2) Mike is able to fix computers.
4. 1) You have to exercise for your health.
   2) Must I finish packing today?

C 보기의 단어를 이용하여 질문을 완성하세요.

보기 sing wear rest pay tell answer park

1. Can I sing a song now? – Yes, you can.
2. ____ I ____ the truth? – Yes, you must.
3. ____ we ____ on the sofa? – No, you can't.
4. ____ you ____ the phone? – Sorry, I can't.
5. ____ I ____ your jacket? – Sure, you may.
6. ____ I ____ my car here? – No, you may not.
7. ____ they ____ the fine? – No, they don't have to.

Words

rest 쉬다
pay 내다, 지불하다
park 주차하다
truth 진실
fine 좋은; 벌금
Japanese 일본어
take medicine 약을 복용하다
chicken 닭
see a doctor 진찰 받다
during ~동안

D 빈칸에 알맞은 말을 써서 대답을 완성하세요.

1. Can you speak Japanese? – Yes, I can.
2. Can he play soccer well? – No, ____.
3. Must I take medicine? – Yes, ____.
4. May I sit here? – Yes, ____.
5. Can chickens fly? – No, ____.
6. Do you have to see a doctor? – No, ____.
7. Can I go out for dinner tonight? – Sorry, ____.
8. May we use our cell phones during the concert?
   – No, ____.

E 우리말과 같은 뜻이 되도록 문장을 완성하고, 보기에서 알맞은 대답을 고르세요.

1. 당신은 빨리 달릴 수 있나요? (can, run)
   → Can you run fast? ⓕ

2. 제가 당신의 휴대폰을 사용해도 될까요? (can, use)
   → ______ your cell phone? ______

3. 그들은 부엌을 치워야 하나요? (must, clean)
   → ______ the kitchen? ______

4. 제가 그 이유를 물어봐도 될까요? (may, ask)
   → ______ the reason? ______

5. 당신은 말을 탈 수 있나요? (be able to, ride)
   → ______ a horse? ______

6. Ethan이 그 전시회에 참석해야 하나요? (have to, attend)
   → ______ the exhibition? ______

7. 그들이 당신의 집에 머물러도 될까요? (can, stay)
   → ______ at your house? ______

8. 내일 보고서를 제출해야 하나요? (must, hand in)
   → ______ my report tomorrow? ______

보기

ⓐ Sorry, they can't.
ⓑ Yes, you must.
ⓒ No, he doesn't have to.
ⓓ No, you may not.
ⓔ Yes, I am. It's exciting.
ⓕ No, I can't.
ⓖ Of course. Here you are.
ⓗ No, they don't have to.

Words

clean 청소하다
ask 묻다
reason 이유
attend 참석하다
exhibition 전시회
stay 머무르다
hand in 제출하다
report 보고서

F 우리말과 같은 뜻이 되도록 밑줄 친 부분을 바르게 고쳐 쓰세요.

1. 당신은 미래를 볼 수 있나요?
   Must you see the future? → Are you able to see
2. 자전거 위에서 헬멧을 써야 하나요?
   Can I wear a helmet on a bike? →
3. 나랑 쇼핑하러 가줄 수 있니?
   May you go shopping with me? →
4. 저 집에 일찍 가도 되나요?
   Do I have to go home early? →
5. 그녀는 호른을 연주할 수 있니?
   May she play the horn? →
6. Sophia는 시험을 봐야 하나요?
   Is Sophia able to take the test? →

Words

future 미래
helmet 헬멧
early 일찍
horn (악기) 호른
turn on (전원을) 켜다
drama club 연극 동아리
arrive 도착하다
on time 제시간에
wear 입다
swimsuit 수영복

G 밑줄 친 부분을 바르게 고쳐 쓰세요.

1. Could you cooks pasta for me? → Could you cook
2. May turn I on the radio? →
3. Can join she our drama club? →
4. Must I took this medicine? →
5. Does Lisa able to arrive on time? →
6. Are we have to wear swimsuits in the pool? →

Grammar into Writing

A 우리말과 같은 뜻이 되도록 주어진 말을 바르게 배열하세요.

1. 제가 도와드릴까요? I / you / help / can

→ Can I help you?

2. 내일 늦게 일어나도 돼요? get up / I / can / late / tomorrow

→ ____________________

3. 제가 음악을 틀어도 될까요? may / the music / turn on / I

→ ____________________

4. 제가 저 채소를 먹어야만 하나요? I / do / have to / those vegetables / eat

→ ____________________

5. 너는 그 책을 이해할 수 있니? you / understand / are / the book / able to

→ ____________________

B 우리말과 같은 뜻이 되도록 주어진 말을 이용하여 문장을 완성하세요.

1. 1) 네 컴퓨터를 써도 되니?

→ May I use your computer?

2) 네 펜을 써도 되니? (pen)

→ May I use your pen?

2. 1) 너는 휘파람을 불 수 있니?

→ ________ ________ whistle?

2) 너는 운전할 수 있니? (drive)

→ ____________________

3. 1) 우리가 교복을 입어야 하나요?

→ ________ ________ wear school uniforms?

2) 제가 체육관에서 운동화를 신어야 하나요? (sneakers, at the gym)

→ ________________________________

4. 1) 설탕 좀 건네주시겠어요?

→ ________ ________ pass me the sugar?

2) 문 좀 열어주시겠어요? (open the door)

→ ________________________________

5. 1) 제가 여기 앉아야 하나요?

→ ________ I ________ ________ sit here?

2) 우리가 여기서 기다려야 하나요? (wait)

→ ________________________________

C 자연스러운 대화가 되도록 밑줄 친 부분을 바르게 고쳐 쓰세요.

A: Excuse me. ❶ May I using my cell phone here?
B: ❷ No, you may. Please use your phone outside.
A: Okay. Can I study with my friends here?
B: Sure. But you ❸ must talk loudly.
A: I know. Can I borrow some books?
B: ❹ Yes, you must. Please wait in line.

↓

❶ May I use ❷ ________________

❸ ________________ ❹ ________________

Words **vegetable** 채소 **whistle** 휘파람을 불다 **sneakers** 운동화 **Excuse me.** 실례합니다. **loudly** 크게 **wait in line** 줄 서서 기다리다

Wrap-Up Test

[1-2] 밑줄 친 말과 의미가 같은 말을 고르세요.

1.

May I take another train?

① Do ② Is ③ Can
④ Must ⑤ Will

2.

Must you do your homework today?

① Can you do ② May you do
③ Would you do ④ Can't you do
⑤ Do you have to do

3. 빈칸에 공통으로 알맞은 것을 고르세요.

• I need the book. ________ you lend it to me? • She looks young. ________ she ride a horse?

① Do ② Can ③ May
④ Must ⑤ Does

4. 두 문장이 같은 의미가 되도록 빈칸에 알맞은 말을 쓰세요.

Can bears run fast? = ________ ________ ________ ________ run fast?

5. 빈칸에 알맞은 말이 바르게 짝지어진 것을 고르세요.

• ________ I get up early tomorrow? (내일 일찍 일어나야 하나요?) • ________ I go to the bathroom? (화장실에 가도 될까요?)

① May – Must ② Can – May
③ Must – May ④ Must – Must
⑤ May – Can

6. 밑줄 친 부분의 의미가 다른 것을 고르세요.

① Can I go now?
② You can come in.
③ Can I eat the cake?
④ Can I use your phone?
⑤ Can you remember her face?

Words **young** 어린 **bear** 곰 **bathroom** 화장실 **come in** 들어오다 **face** 얼굴

7. 빈칸에 알맞은 말을 고르세요.

A: ____________________

B: No, you don't have to.

① Do I go to the library?

② Can I go to the library?

③ May I go to the library?

④ Must I go to the library?

⑤ Am I able to go to the library?

8. 우리말과 영어가 잘못 짝지어진 것을 고르세요.

① 제가 그에게 전화해야 하나요?
→ May I call him?

② 당신의 가족사진을 봐도 될까요?
→ Can I see a picture of your family?

③ 우리 집에 와 줄래요?
→ Could you come to my house?

④ 제가 그 수업을 들어야 하나요?
→ Do I have to take the class?

⑤ 그녀는 영어를 말할 수 있나요?
→ Is she able to speak English?

9. 밑줄 친 부분을 바르게 고친 것을 고르시오.

Does she has to prepare that food now?

① Must she prepare

② Must she prepares

③ Do she has to prepare

④ Do she have to prepare

⑤ Does she have to prepares

10. 대화가 어색한 것을 고르세요.

① A: May I look at the map?
B: Sure. Here you are.

② A: Must I send him an e-mail?
B: Yes, you must.

③ A: Can we go out for dinner tonight?
B: Of course.

④ A: Can you lend me some money?
B: Sorry, you can't.

⑤ A: Is he able to kick the ball?
B: Yes, he is.

Words **take a class** 수업을 듣다 **prepare** 준비하다 **map** 지도 **kick** (발로) 차다

서술형

11. 틀린 문장을 고르세요.

① Can I get some water?

② May I borrow your textbook?

③ Can she plays tennis well?

④ Do we have to take a taxi?

⑤ Are you able to drive a car?

[12-13] 대화를 읽고, 물음에 답하세요.

A: ① May I help you?

B: Yes. I want to register for your lessons.

A: Welcome! You can register now.

B: Great. ② Can I take a lesson today?

A: I'm sorry, ③ you can. But tomorrow's class is okay.

B: Then I'll come tomorrow. ④ May I bring my friend?

A: ⑤ Sure! 하지만 늦어서는 안 돼요.

12. 밑줄 친 부분이 어색한 것을 고르세요.

① ② ③ ④ ⑤

서술형

13. 밑줄 친 우리말과 같은 뜻이 되도록 빈칸에 알맞은 말을 쓰세요.

But you ________ ________ ________ late.

서술형

14. 우리말과 같은 뜻이 되도록 주어진 말을 이용하여 문장을 완성하세요.

제가 안전벨트를 꼭 매야 하나요?
(have to, wear a seat belt)

→ ____________________
____

서술형

15. 우리말과 같은 뜻이 되도록 빈칸에 알맞은 말을 쓰세요. (빈칸에 한 단어씩 쓸 것)

A: ________ ________ take my dog with me?
(제 개를 데리고 가도 될까요?)

B: Sure, but you ________ leave him alone.
(물론이죠, 하지만 혼자 두어서는 안 돼요.)

Words **textbook** 교과서 **register** 등록하다 **lesson** 수업, 강습 **welcome** 환영하다 **seat belt** 안전벨트

UNIT 07

부사

Vocab Check! 이번 과에서 배울 단어의 뜻을 확인하고, 모르는 단어에 체크 표시하세요.

1	lately	부 최근에
2	friendly	형 친한, 친절한
3	sorry	형 미안한
4	lovely	형 사랑스러운
5	explain	동 설명하다
6	grammar	명 문법
7	fortunate	형 운 좋은
8	become	동 ~이 되다
9	feel	동 느끼다
10	honestly	부 솔직히
11	perform	동 수행하다
12	final	형 마지막의
13	moving	형 감동적인
14	stomach	명 배
15	safe	형 안전한
16	simple	형 간단한
17	suddenly	부 갑자기
18	laugh	동 웃다
19	peaceful	형 평화로운
20	politely	부 공손하게
21	brightly	부 밝게
22	title	명 제목
23	lazy	형 게으른
24	grow up	자라다
25	believe	동 믿다
26	busy	형 바쁜
27	cheerful	형 쾌활한
28	airplane	명 비행기
29	princess	명 공주
30	mermaid	명 인어

UNIT 07 부사

Rabbit is running **slowly**. Turtle is walking **fast**.
토끼는 천천히 뛰고 있어요. 거북은 빨리 걷고 있어요.

Finally, Turtle wins the race.
마침내, 거북은 경주에서 이겨요.

Turtle smiles **happily**.
거북은 행복하게 미소 지어요.

A 부사의 의미와 종류

부사는 문장의 의미를 더 풍부하게 만들어줘요.
부사는 기본적으로 '~하게'라고 해석하지만, 아래와 같이 다양해요.

시간	today (오늘) now (지금) yesterday (어제) tomorrow (내일) soon (곧)
장소	here (여기에(서), 여기로) there (거기에(서), 거기로) outside (밖에(서))
방법, 정도	loudly (큰 소리로) happily (행복하게) kindly (친절하게) safely (안전하게) fast (빨리) well (잘) very (매우) really (정말) so (너무)
빈도, 횟수	always (항상) often (종종, 자주) sometimes (가끔) never (결코 ~않다) once (한 번)

-le로 끝나는 형용사는 -le를 -ly로 바꿔요.
simple (간단한) - simply (그저, 단순히)

B 부사의 형태

대부분의 부사	형용사+ly	nice (멋진) → nicely (멋지게) sad (슬픈) → sadly (슬프게) careful (조심스러운) → carefully (조심스럽게)
y로 끝나는 형용사	y 대신 -ily	easy (쉬운) → easily (쉽게) happy (행복한) → happily (행복하게) lucky (운이 좋은) → luckily (운 좋게)
형용사와 형태가 같은 부사	fast (빠른) – **fast** (빨리) early (이른) – **early** (일찍) late (늦은) – **late** (늦게) high (높은) – **high** (높게) hard (어려운, 힘든) – **hard** (열심히)	
예외	good (좋은) – **well** (잘, 좋게)	

late와 hard에 -ly를 붙이면 각각
lately(최근에)와 hardly(거의 ~ 아니다)라는
전혀 다른 뜻의 부사가 되니 주의하세요.

C 부사의 역할

부사는 아래와 같이 명사를 제외한 여러 요소를 꾸며 줍니다.

be동사와 감각동사(sound, smell, look, taste, feel) 뒤에는 부사가 아닌 형용사를 써요.
She looks **beautiful**. (O)
(그녀는 아름다워 보여요.)
She looks beautifully. (X)

1. **동사 수식:** 부사가 동사 뒤에서 동사를 꾸며줘요.

동사 + 부사

I get up **early**.
He studies **hard**.

2. **형용사 수식:** 부사가 형용사 앞에서 형용사를 꾸며줘요.

부사 + 형용사

We are **really** good friends.
This comic book is **very** interesting.

3. **부사 수식:** 부사는 다른 부사 앞에서 그 부사를 꾸며주기도 해요.

부사 + 부사

He can run **very** fast.
My sister swims **very** well.

4. **문장 전체 수식:** 부사는 문장의 맨 앞에서 전체 문장의 의미를 꾸며주기도 해요.

부사 + 문장

Sadly, we lost the baseball game.
Suddenly, the rain stopped.

My Grammar Notes

1 __________는 문장의 의미를 풍부하게 만들어 주는 말이다.

2 부사의 형태

(1) 형용사+ly: sad → __________
(2) -y를 i로 바꾸고+ly: happy → __________
(3) __________와 같은 형태: fast - fast
(4) 예외: good - __________

3 부사는 동사, 형용사, 부사, 문장 전체의 의미를 꾸며준다.

(1) walk slowly (__________ 수식)
(2) so beautiful (__________ 수식)
(3) very well (__________ 수식)
(4) Luckily, they found the key. (문장 전체 수식)

Warm-Up

A 다음 중에서 부사를 고르세요. 부사의 형태

1. ① here ② great ③ music ④ eat
2. ① big ② see ③ well ④ cook
3. ① study ② kindly ③ sick ④ friendly
4. ① early ② difficult ③ have ④ soft
5. ① sorry ② poor ③ very ④ expensive
6. ① always ② keep ③ place ④ quiet
7. ① hurt ② lucky ③ fat ④ soon
8. ① worry ② now ③ lovely ④ hurry

B 다음 문장에서 부사를 찾아 O 표시하세요. 부사의 역할

1. I can open the lid easily.
2. I can jump high.
3. I'll call you tonight.
4. You must try hard to be healthy.
5. Can you wait for me outside?
6. The movie was really exciting.
7. Luckily, they passed the exam.
8. Is the train traveling fast?

Words

friendly 친한, 친절한
soft 부드러운
sorry 미안한
expensive 비싼
hurt 아프다, 다치게 하다
lucky 운이 좋은
worry 걱정하다
lovely 사랑스러운
lid 뚜껑
try 노력하다
healthy 건강한
exciting 흥미로운
pass the exam 시험에 합격하다

C 주어진 형용사의 부사형을 쓰고, 그 뜻을 바르게 연결하세요. 부사의 형태

1. sad	sadly	•	• ⓐ 아름답게
2. beautiful		•	• ⓑ 가볍게
3. light		•	• ⓒ 슬프게
4. quiet		•	• ⓓ 좋게, 잘
5. easy		•	• ⓔ 쉽게
6. careful		•	• ⓕ 빠르게
7. fast		•	• ⓖ 조심스럽게
8. good		•	• ⓗ 조용하게
9. nice		•	• ⓘ 멋지게

Words

light 가벼운
quiet 조용한
careful 주의 깊은
title 제목
honestly 솔직히
smile 미소 짓다
brightly 밝게
lazy 게으른

D 밑줄 친 부사가 꾸미는 말을 찾아 쓰세요. 부사의 역할

1. Please read the title <u>loudly</u>. read
2. This garden is <u>so</u> beautiful.
3. He studies <u>very</u> hard.
4. She always gets up <u>early</u>.
5. <u>Honestly</u>, I don't like him.
6. The baby smiles <u>brightly</u>.
7. Juliet is a <u>very</u> lazy girl.
8. Those students talk <u>too</u> much.

Practice

A 보기와 같은 관계가 되도록 빈칸에 알맞은 단어를 쓰세요.

보기 happy – happily

1. quick → quickly
2. early →
3. cheerful →
4. busy →
5. fast →
6. lucky →
7. good →
8. sad →
9. recent →
10. loud →
11. safe →
12. soft →
13. simple →
14. fortunate →
15. gentle →
16. peaceful →

Words

quick 빠른
cheerful 쾌활한
busy 바쁜
recent 최근의
safe 안전한
simple 간단한
fortunate 운 좋은
gentle 온화한, 점잖은
peaceful 평화로운
sing 노래하다 (과거형 **sang**)
frog 개구리
move 옮기다
these days 요즘
answer 대답하다

B 우리말과 같은 뜻이 되도록 ( ) 안에서 알맞은 것을 고르세요.

1. 그들은 천천히 걸었다. They walked (slowly / shortly).
2. 그녀는 행복하게 노래했다. She sang (happily / nicely).
3. 개구리는 높이 뛸 수 있다. Frogs can jump (high / highly).
4. 나는 빠르게 상자를 옮겼다. I moved the box (quietly / quickly).
5. 그는 요즘 열심히 공부한다. He studies (hard / much) these days.
6. 그 소녀는 친절하게 대답했다. The girl answered (clearly / kindly).

C ( ) 안에서 알맞은 것을 고르세요.

1. Sumi is (real / really) cute.
2. I feel (happy / happily) now.
3. She arrived (late / lately) today.
4. This music sounds (nice / nicely).
5. Sam learns English (quick / quickly).
6. Tommy is a (good / well) soccer player.
7. (Sudden / Suddenly), the room became dark.
8. We can find many restaurants (easy / easily) at the mall.

Words

feel 느끼다
sound ~하게 들리다
become ~이 되다, ~해지다 (과거형 **became**)
dark 어두운
worker 일하는 사람, 노동자
cook 요리사; 요리하다
driver 운전자
princess 공주
life 인생, 삶

D 두 문장의 의미가 통하도록 빈칸에 알맞은 말을 쓰세요.

1. He is a hard worker.
→ He works hard.
2. Peter is a fast runner.
→ Peter runs ______.
3. Betty has a beautiful smile.
→ Betty smiles ______.
4. My sister is a good cook.
→ My sister cooks ______.
5. Allen is a careful driver.
→ Allen drives ______.
6. Shrek and Princess Fiona lived a happy life.
→ Shrek and Princess Fiona lived ______.

E 우리말과 같은 뜻이 되도록 보기의 단어를 활용하여 문장을 완성하세요. (필요하면 단어의 형태를 바꾸세요.)

보기	quiet	easy	lucky	real	quick
	sudden	sad	loud	late	good

1. 그들은 진짜로 UFO의 존재를 믿었다.
   → They really believed in UFOs.
2. 그 아이들은 큰 소리로 울고 있다.
   → The children are crying ________.
3. 우리 아빠는 컴퓨터를 쉽게 고칠 수 있다.
   → My father can fix computers ________.
4. 잘 잤니?
   → Did you sleep ________?
5. Tim은 항상 수업에 늦게 온다.
   → Tim always comes to class ________.
6. 운이 좋게도, 그는 복권에 당첨되었다.
   → ________, he won the lottery.
7. 그는 갑자기 비행기 안에서 속이 메스꺼웠다.
   → He ________ felt sick on the airplane.
8. 그들은 교실에서 조용히 이야기하고 있다.
   → They are talking ________ in the classroom.
9. Amelia는 그 집에서 빠르게 도망쳐 나왔다.
   → Amelia ran out of the house ________.
10. 슬프게도, 그 뉴스는 사실이었다.
   → ________, the news was true.

Words

believe 믿다
UFO 미확인 비행 물체
fix 고치다, 수리하다
win the lottery 복권에 당첨되다
feel sick (속이) 메스껍다
airplane 비행기
run out of ~에서 달아나다
true 사실인, 맞는

F 밑줄 친 부분을 바르게 고쳐 쓰세요.

1. The birds can fly <u>highly</u>. →
2. Spend your money <u>wise</u>. →
3. He <u>early arrived</u> to the meeting. →
4. My uncle bought a truck <u>recent</u>. →
5. Kate always studies <u>hardly</u>. →
6. I understand you <u>perfect</u>. →
7. <u>Honest</u>, I didn't remember her name. →
8. The books are selling <u>fastly</u>. →

G <u>틀린</u> 부분을 찾아 바르게 고쳐 쓰세요.

1. The mermaid swims very good. good → well
2. Sudden, the car stopped. →
3. Dr. Smith is a well doctor. →
4. Final, he came back. →
5. You must be politely to people. →
6. I got up lately this morning. →
7. Today, the sky is clear very. →
8. This cake tastes greatly. →

Words

spend (돈 등을) 쓰다
wise 현명한
arrive 도착하다
truck 트럭
understand 이해하다
perfect 완벽한
remember 기억하다
sell 팔다; 팔리다
mermaid 인어
stop 멈추다
final 마지막의, 결국의
politely 공손하게, 예의 바르게
clear 맑은
taste ~한 맛이 나다

Grammar into Writing

A 우리말과 같은 뜻이 되도록 어울리는 것끼리 선으로 연결하고, 문장을 만드세요.

1. He always drives. •	• ⓐ very
2. Kids grow up. •	• ⓑ fortunately
3. He got a free ticket. •	• ⓒ quickly
4. She arrived at the hotel. •	• ⓓ early
5. I am busy today. •	• ⓔ gently
6. You must listen to me. •	• ⓕ carefully

1. 그는 항상 점잖게 운전한다.

→ He always drives gently.

2. 아이들은 빨리 자란다.

→

3. 운이 좋게도, 그는 무료 티켓을 얻었다.

→

4. 그녀는 호텔에 일찍 도착했다.

→

5. 나는 오늘 매우 바쁘다.

→

6. 너는 내 말을 주의 깊게 들어야 한다.

→

B 우리말과 같은 뜻이 되도록 주어진 말을 이용하여 문장을 만드세요.

1. 그녀는 수학 공부를 열심히 했다. (study math)

→ She studied math hard.

2. 그가 밖에서 너를 기다리고 있어. (wait for you)

→ ______

3. Eric은 말을 매우 잘 탄다. (ride a horse)

→ ______

4. Sally는 질문에 친절하게 대답했다. (answer the question)

→ ______

5. 나는 조용히 그 문을 열었다. (open the door)

→ ______

C 다음 글을 읽고, 틀린 부분을 찾아 표시한 다음, 바르게 고쳐 쓰세요.

I'm a baby kangaroo. I live in a pocket on my mom's stomach. The pocket is very largely and cozy. My mom always carries me in her pocket safe. She can hop really highly. So, lucky, I can go everywhere with her.

1. largely → large 2. ______ → ______

3. ______ → ______ 4. ______ → ______

Words
grow up 자라다 **free** 무료의, 공짜의 **kangaroo** 캥거루 **pocket** 주머니
stomach 배 **cozy** 편안한 **carry** 가지고 다니다, 데리고 있다 **hop** 깡충깡충 뛰다
everywhere 어디든지

Wrap-Up Test

1. 빈칸에 들어갈 수 <u>없는</u> 것을 고르세요.

You can do the job __________.

① now ② fast
③ easily ④ good
⑤ here

2. 짝지어진 단어의 관계가 나머지와 <u>다른</u> 것을 고르세요.

① sad – sadly ② luck – lucky
③ safe – safely ④ careful – carefully
⑤ gentle – gently

[3-4] 빈칸에 공통으로 들어갈 말을 고르세요.

3.

• I practiced __________ for the audition.
• It was very __________ work for me.

① hard ② lazy
③ soon ④ many
⑤ well

4.

• I was __________ for the concert.
• Did you study __________ at night?

① nicely ② busy
③ late ④ cheerful
⑤ softly

5. 밑줄 친 부분이 부사로 쓰인 것을 <u>모두</u> 고르세요. (3개)

① Look at the <u>lovely</u> baby!
② I <u>often</u> bake some cookies.
③ Do you want to be <u>healthy</u>?
④ Those birds cannot fly <u>high</u>.
⑤ The man performed magic <u>perfectly</u>.

서술형

6. 두 문장이 서로 반대 의미가 되도록 빈칸에 알맞은 말을 쓰세요.

They sang the song quietly.
↔ They sang the song __________.

Words **job** 일, 직업 **audition** 오디션 **often** 종종, 자주 **perform** 수행하다 **magic** 마법, 마술

[7-8] 빈칸에 알맞은 말이 바르게 짝지어진 것을 고르세요.

7.

- I work __________ at night these days.
- They want __________ delivery.

① late – quick ② late – quickly
③ late – lately ④ lately – quickly
⑤ quick – quickly

8.

- __________, Olivia lost her job.
- He feels very __________.
- The cars go __________ fast.

① Recent – happy – real
② Recent – happily – really
③ Recently – happy – real
④ Recently – happily – really
⑤ Recently – happy – really

9. 밑줄 친 부사의 역할이 보기와 같은 것을 고르세요.

보기 This comic book is very interesting.

① Finally, I met her again.
② You have to get up early.
③ The movie was really moving.
④ Jihoon ran so fast in the race.
⑤ He came to the museum very late.

10. 우리말과 영어가 잘못 짝지어진 것을 고르세요.

① 그녀는 높이 뛸 수 있다.
→ She can jump highly.
② 그는 거의 운동하지 않는다.
→ He hardly works out.
③ 슬프게도, 그녀의 개가 죽었다.
→ Sadly, her dog died.
④ 내 여동생은 매우 아름답다.
→ My sister is very beautiful.
⑤ 이 책은 문법을 간단하게 설명한다.
→ This book explains grammar simply.

Words **delivery** 배달 **lose** 잃다 (과거형 **lost**) **moving** 감동적인 **race** 경주 **museum** 박물관 **work out** 운동하다 **explain** 설명하다 **grammar** 문법

11. 밑줄 친 부분이 올바른 것을 고르세요.

① He is an <u>honestly</u> boy.

② The pasta tastes <u>greatly</u>.

③ The plane flies <u>lowly</u>.

④ She has a very <u>useful</u> tool.

⑤ My neighbor talked to me <u>friendly</u>.

12. 다음 중 <u>틀린</u> 문장을 고르세요.

① He plays the piano very well.

② Let's eat out today.

③ Suddenly, my brother started to laugh.

④ I can answer the question easy.

⑤ The woman looks kind and polite.

서술형

13. 두 문장이 같은 뜻이 되도록 빈칸에 알맞은 말을 쓰세요.

My father is a very slow taxi driver.
= The taxi driver drives __________ __________.

서술형

14. 우리말과 같은 뜻이 되도록 주어진 단어를 사용하여 문장을 완성하세요.

A: Christine, <u>당신은 한국말을 잘하는군요.</u> (speak Korean)
B: Yes. I learned it from my mother. She is Korean.

→ ______________________________

서술형

15. <u>틀린</u> 부분을 찾아 바르게 고쳐 쓰세요. (2개)

Fortunate, she caught the lastly train.

→ ______________________________

Words useful 유용한 tool 도구 neighbor 이웃

UNIT 08

빈도부사

Vocab Check! 이번 과에서 배울 단어의 뜻을 확인하고, 모르는 단어에 체크 표시하세요.

1 absent 형 결석한	11 experiment 명 실험	21 fall asleep 잠들다
2 subject 명 과목	12 bite 동 물다	22 try one's best 최선을 다하다
3 story 명 이야기	13 cash 명 현금	23 junk food 명 정크푸드
4 forget 동 잊다	14 rise 동 떠오르다	24 say sorry 사과하다
5 draw a picture 그림을 그리다	15 east 명 동쪽	25 plant 동 심다 명 식물
6 soldier 명 군인	16 cover 동 덮다	26 strangely 부 이상하게
7 break 명 휴식	17 freeze 동 얼다	27 take out 꺼내다
8 spend 동 (시간을) 보내다	18 badminton 명 배드민턴	28 smog 명 스모그, 연무
9 activity 명 활동	19 act 동 행동하다	29 depend on ~에 의지하다
10 history 명 역사	20 magazine 명 잡지	30 on foot 걸어서

UNIT 08 빈도부사

Tony always goes to bed late.
토니는 항상 늦게 잠자리에 들어요.

But he never gets up late.
하지만 그는 절대 늦게 일어나지 않아요.

He usually takes a nap in the afternoon.
그는 보통 오후에 낮잠을 자요.

A 빈도부사의 의미와 종류

빈도부사는 어떤 일이 얼마나 자주 일어나는지 나타내는 말로, 자주 사용하는 빈도부사에는 다음과 같은 것들이 있어요.

always	usually	often	sometimes	never
(언제나, 항상)	(대개, 보통)	(종종, 자주)	(가끔, 때때로)	(절대 ~않는)

100% ← → 0%

B 빈도부사의 위치

1. be동사와 조동사 뒤

He **is**	always	kind and gentle. (be동사)
It **is**	usually	sunny in L.A. (be동사)
I **am**	often	late for my piano lesson. (be동사)
You **may**	sometimes	borrow my books. (조동사)
We **must**	never	smoke in this building. (조동사)

never에는 부정의 의미가 있기 때문에 not과 함께 쓰지 않아요.
I'm not never late for school. (X)
I'm **never** late for school. (O)

2. 일반동사 앞

I	always	**take** a walk after dinner.
Patrick	usually	**drinks** coffee in the café.
They	often	**go** camping in summer.
Mrs. Brown	sometimes	**helps** poor people.
We	never	**study** on Sunday.

C how often 의문문

어떤 일이 얼마나 자주 일어나는지를 물을 때는 how often(얼마나 자주)을 사용해요.
답변할 때는 빈도를 나타내는 여러 가지 표현을 이용해요.

질문		
How often (얼마나 자주)	be동사	주어 ~?
	do / does	주어 + 동사원형 ~?
	조동사	

→

대답
빈도를 나타내는 표현 (빈도부사 / every Sunday (일요일마다), / twice a week (일주일에 두 번) 등)

How often are you late for school? – I am **never** late for school.

How often does she exercise? – She **sometimes** exercises.
– She goes to the gym **every Sunday**.

My Grammar Notes

1 빈도부사: 어떤 일이 얼마나 자주 일어나는지를 나타내는 말

always	________	often	________	________

100% ←――――――――――――――――→ 0%

2 빈도부사는 be동사와 ________ 뒤에, ________ 앞에 쓴다.

3 ________ ________은 '얼마나 자주'의 뜻으로 빈도를 물을 때 쓴다.
대답할 때는 빈도부사나 every Sunday, once a week와 같은 표현을 이용한다.
________ ________ do you go shopping? – Twice a month.
(당신은 얼마나 자주 쇼핑하러 가나요?) (한 달에 두 번이요.)

Warm-Up

A 빈도부사를 찾아 O 표시하세요. 빈도부사의 종류

1. I will never forget your birthday.
2. I usually go to bed at 9 o'clock.
3. Tom sometimes lies to me.
4. My teacher often tells us funny stories.
5. Our family always eats out on Sundays.
6. I often feel tired these days.

B 우리말과 같은 뜻이 되도록 ( ) 안에서 알맞은 것을 고르세요.

빈도부사의 종류

1. 군인은 항상 총을 가지고 다닌다.
   → Soldiers (always / often) carry their guns.
2. 그는 종종 늦게 일어난다.
   → He (often / never) gets up late.
3. 우리는 가끔 휴식이 필요하다.
   → We (usually / sometimes) need a break.
4. 너는 그를 절대 믿을 수 없다.
   → You can (always / never) trust him.
5. 나는 보통 토요일에 낚시를 간다.
   → I (usually / never) go fishing on Saturday.
6. 그 의사는 가끔 양로원에서 자원봉사를 한다.
   → The doctor (sometimes / always) does volunteer work at a nursing home.

Words

forget 잊다
lie 거짓말하다
funny 재미있는
story 이야기
eat out 외식하다
soldier 군인
carry 가지고 다니다
gun 총
need 필요하다
break 휴식
trust 믿다
do volunteer work 자원봉사를 하다
nursing home 양로원

C 빈도부사가 들어갈 위치로 알맞은 것을 고르세요. 빈도부사의 위치

1. always — Laura ① is ② friendly.
2. sometimes — You ① act ② strangely.
3. always — I will ① love ② you.
4. usually — I ① go ② to school by bus.
5. never — He is ① late ② for meetings.
6. often — How ① do ② you go to the gym?
7. often — She ① forgets ② my telephone number.
8. never — At night, Mrs. Kim ① shows ② her children TV programs.

Words

friendly 친절한
act 행동하다
strangely 이상하게
be late for ~에 늦다
meeting 회의
gym 체육관
show 보여주다
take a test 시험을 보다

D 질문에 알맞은 대답을 연결하세요. how often 의문문

1. How often do you go shopping? •
2. How often do we have to take a test? •
3. How often do you go to the movies? •
4. How often do you play tennis? •
5. How often does the bus leave? •

• ⓐ There's a test once a month.
• ⓑ I play tennis every weekend.
• ⓒ I sometimes go shopping.
• ⓓ It leaves every 5 minutes.
• ⓔ I see a movie every Friday night.

Practice

A ( ) 안에서 알맞은 것을 고르세요.

1. You (always must / must always) try your best.
2. My uncle (often takes / takes often) me to the zoo.
3. He (never gets / gets never) angry in any situation.
4. She (always goes / goes always) outside on weekends.
5. You (sometimes can / can sometimes) have dinner with me.
6. Dan (never arrives / arrives never) late for his swimming lesson.
7. We (usually spend / spend usually) our free time at the beach.

Words

try one's best 최선을 다하다
angry 화가 난
in any situation 어떤 상황에서도
lesson 강습
spend (시간을) 보내다
free time 자유 시간
beach 해변
bark 짖다
bite 물다

B 자주 일어나는 일부터 순서대로 배열하세요.

1. ① He often has breakfast.
② He usually gets up early.
③ He always takes the school bus.
③ → ② → ①

2. ① My sister never lies to me.
② My sister sometimes helps me.
③ My sister is always kind to people.
→ →

3. ① Tom usually exercises at the gym.
② Tom never plays the piano.
③ Tom sometimes watches TV at home.
→ →

4. ① My dog sometimes barks.
② My dog never bites people.
③ My dog often sleeps under the table.
→ →

C 표를 보고, 내용과 일치하는 문장에는 T, 그렇지 않으면 F를 쓰세요.

School Schedule

	Monday	Tuesday	Wednesday	Thursday	Friday
Subject	English, Math	Science, Math	Science, English, Math	English, Math, Music	History, Math
After-school Activity	baseball game	volunteer work	baseball game	science experiment	baseball game

1. He never attends history class. F
2. He always takes a math class.
3. He sometimes does volunteer work.
4. He often plays baseball after school.
5. He always does a science experiment.

D 밑줄 친 부분을 바르게 고쳐 쓰세요.

1. He gets usually sick. → usually gets
2. I will be never absent again. →
3. How often you go to church? →
4. You must tell always the truth. →
5. She forgets sometimes the password. →
6. Do usually Americans eat turkey on Thanksgiving Day?
→

Words

schedule 스케줄, 일정
subject 과목
history 역사
activity 활동
experiment 실험
attend 참석하다
sick 아픈
absent 결석한
church 교회
truth 진실, 사실
password 비밀번호
turkey 칠면조
Thanksgiving Day 추수감사절

E 주어진 대답에 알맞은 질문을 보기에서 고르세요.

보기
ⓐ Do you always carry a wallet?
ⓑ How often do you eat breakfast?
ⓒ Is Dave often late for school?
ⓓ How often does Nick play computer games?

1. ⓑ – I always eat breakfast.
2. ____ – Yes, I do. I always need some cash.
3. ____ – He plays computer games every day.
4. ____ – No. He is never late for school.

Words

carry 가지고 다니다
wallet 지갑
cash 현금
junk food 정크푸드, 패스트푸드
download 다운로드하다
almost 거의

F 주어진 말을 이용하여 질문에 대한 대답을 쓰세요.

1. A: How often do they eat junk food? (three times a week)
   B: They eat junk food three times a week.
2. A: How often can I download music? (always)
   B: ____
3. A: How often does she go to dance parties? (never)
   B: ____
4. A: How often do you climb mountains? (once a year)
   B: ____
5. A: How often does it rain in London? (almost every day)
   B: ____

G 우리말과 같은 뜻이 되도록 주어진 말을 이용하여 문장을 완성하세요.

1. 나는 늘 당신을 기억할 것입니다. (will, remember)
→ I will always remember you.

2. 그녀는 결코 내 말을 듣지 않는다. (listen)
→ She ______ to me.

3. 우리 아빠는 때때로 낚시를 하러 가신다. (go)
→ My father ______ fishing.

4. 내 여동생은 언제나 쾌활하다. (be)
→ My little sister ______ cheerful.

5. Blair는 절대 미안하다고 말하지 않을 것이다. (will, say)
→ Blair ______ sorry.

6. 해는 항상 동쪽에서 떠오른다. (rise)
→ The sun ______ in the east.

7. 너는 언제든지 우리 집에 올 수 있다. (can, come)
→ You ______ to my house.

8. 나는 대개 정오에 점심을 먹는다. (have)
→ I ______ lunch at noon.

9. 너는 얼마나 자주 영화를 보러 가니? (go)
→ ______ to the movies?

10. Paul은 얼마나 자주 이 수영장에서 수영하니? (swim)
→ ______ in this swimming pool?

11. 스모그가 때때로 서울 전체를 뒤덮는다. (cover)
→ Smog ______ all of Seoul.

12. 너희는 크리스마스에 보통 무엇을 하니? (what, do)
→ ______ on Christmas?

Words

cheerful 쾌활한
say sorry 사과하다
rise 떠오르다
east 동쪽
at noon 정오에
swimming pool 수영장
cover 덮다
smog 스모그, 연무

Grammar into Writing

A 우리말과 같은 뜻이 되도록 두 보기에서 각각 알맞은 말을 골라 문장을 만드세요.

보기				
never	sometimes	always	often	usually

보기 freeze in winter / fall asleep in class / be busy in the morning / go to bed at 10 / see horror movies / must be careful on roads / take a nap after lunch / buy a gift for my little brother

1. 운전자들은 도로에서 항상 조심해야 한다.
   → Drivers __must always be careful on roads__.
2. 그 강은 겨울에 가끔 언다.
   → The river ________________.
3. Daniel은 가끔 수업 시간에 잠이 든다.
   → ________________
4. 나는 항상 점심 식사 후 낮잠을 잔다.
   → ________________
5. Brian은 보통 10시에 잠자리에 든다.
   → ________________
6. 나는 종종 남동생에게 선물을 사준다.
   → ________________
7. 그녀는 절대 공포 영화를 보지 않는다.
   → ________________
8. 그들은 아침에 항상 바쁘다.
   → ________________

B 우리말과 같은 뜻이 되도록 주어진 말을 바르게 배열하세요.

1. 그는 오후에 보통 도서관에 간다. goes to / usually / he / the library

→ He usually goes to the library in the afternoon.

2. Alice는 수업 시간에 절대 늦지 않을 것이다. never / late for / be / Alice / will

→ ______________________ class.

3. 당신은 얼마나 자주 여행을 가나요? you / how / go / do / often

→ ______________________ on trips?

4. 나는 항상 너에게 이메일을 보낼 수 있어. can / e-mails / send / I / always

→ ______________________ to you.

5. 그녀는 때때로 센트럴 파크에서 산책을 한다. takes a walk / sometimes / she

→ ______________________ in Central Park.

C 다음 글을 읽고 틀린 부분을 찾아 표시한 다음, 고쳐서 다시 써보세요.

Sean always is busy every morning. He must get on the school bus. The school bus usually arrive at 8 a.m. But it sometimes is 10 minutes late. How often do he miss the bus? Never! On the bus, he sits often next to his best friend Rolla.

↓

Sean is always busy every morning.

____

____

Words **freeze** 얼다 **fall asleep** 잠들다 **take a nap** 낮잠을 자다 **go on a trip** 여행을 가다 **take a walk** 산책하다 **get on** ~에 타다 **miss** 놓치다

Wrap-Up Test

[1-2] 주어진 빈도부사가 들어갈 위치를 고르세요.

1.

He ① watches ② his ③ favorite ④ TV show ⑤ at night. (sometimes)

2.

You ① can ② take ③ a walk ④ with your dog ⑤ in the morning. (always)

3. 빈도부사가 들어갈 위치가 잘못 표시된 것을 고르세요.

① I'm√late for meetings.

② She√reads magazines.

③ You must help√others.

④ We√visit the National Museum.

⑤ They will√take out the trash.

4. 빈칸에 알맞은 것을 고르세요.

Junsu ________________ late on Saturdays.

① gets up usually

② gets often up

③ always get up

④ get never up

⑤ sometimes gets up

5. 빈칸에 들어갈 수 없는 것을 고르세요.

A: How often do you exercise?

B: ________________

① Every day. ② Once a week.

③ Yes, I do. ④ I never exercise.

⑤ I exercise on weekends.

6. 가장 자주 하는 일부터 순서대로 나열하세요.

① Andy usually draws a picture.

② Andy sometimes listens to music.

③ Andy always reads a newspaper.

________ → ________ → ________

Words **magazine** 잡지 **national museum** 국립 박물관 **take out** 꺼내다 **trash** 쓰레기 **draw a picture** 그림을 그리다 **newspaper** 신문

7. 우리말을 영어로 바르게 옮긴 것을 고르세요.

나는 절대로 우유를 마시지 않을 것이다.

① I will never drink milk.

② I will drink milk never.

③ I will drink never milk.

④ I will not never drink milk.

⑤ I will never not drink milk.

8. 밑줄 친 부분을 바르게 고친 것을 고르세요.

- Alex <u>never do</u> his homework.
- A good friend <u>will listen always</u> to you.

① does never – will always listen

② does never – will listen always

③ do never – will always listen

④ never does – will listen always

⑤ never does – will always listen

9. 영어와 우리말이 잘못 짝지어진 것을 고르세요.

① I never jog in the morning.
→ 나는 절대 아침에 조깅하지 않는다.

② She sometimes goes to see a movie.
→ 그녀는 항상 영화를 보러 간다.

③ He usually plays soccer on Sunday.
→ 그는 보통 일요일에 축구를 한다.

④ How often do you meet your aunt?
→ 너는 얼마나 자주 이모를 만나니?

⑤ You must often call your grandmother.
→ 너는 종종 할머니께 전화를 드려야 한다.

10. 틀린 문장을 고르세요.

① I often surf the internet.

② You can always depend on me.

③ She sometimes watches TV at home.

④ Chris isn't never happy.

⑤ They usually help the poor.

Words
jog 조깅하다 **surf the internet** 인터넷을 검색하다 **depend on** ~를 믿다, ~에 의지하다
the poor 가난한 사람들

11. 대화가 어색한 것을 고르세요.

① A: Are you never late for school?
   B: No. I'm sometimes late for school.

② A: How often do you ride a bike?
   B: I ride a bike twice a week.

③ A: What do you usually do after school?
   B: I play badminton with my sister.

④ A: Do you usually go to school by bus?
   B: No. I go to school on foot.

⑤ A: How often does Jenny go shopping?
   B: She'll go shopping today.

[12-13] 우리말과 같은 뜻이 되도록 주어진 말을 바르게 배열하세요.

서술형

12.

그는 대개 수학에서 좋은 점수를 받는다.
(gets / grades in math / usually / he / good)

→ ______________________________

____

서술형

13.

그녀는 얼마나 자주 게임을 할 수 있니?
(games / how / can / play / she / often)

→ ______________________________

____

서술형

14. 우리말과 같은 뜻이 되도록 주어진 말을 이용하여 문장을 완성하세요.

너희는 항상 하루에 세 번 이를 닦아야 한다.
(brush your teeth)

→ You ________ ________ ________ ________ ________ three times a day.

서술형

15. 틀린 부분을 찾아 바르게 고쳐 쓰세요.

You can give sometimes some water to the plants.

________ → ________

Words badminton 배드민턴 on foot 걸어서 grade 성적, 점수 plant 식물

UNIT 09

숫자 표현

Vocab Check! 이번 과에서 배울 단어의 뜻을 확인하고, 모르는 단어에 체크 표시하세요.

1	invitation	명 초대(장)	11	item	명 물건, 물품	21	delicious	형 맛있는
2	charity	명 자선	12	donate	동 기부하다	22	rotten	형 썩은
3	event	명 행사, 이벤트	13	survive	동 살아남다	23	participant	명 참가자
4	guest	명 손님	14	daughter	명 딸	24	last	동 지속되다
5	director	명 감독	15	middle school	명 중학교	25	hospital	명 병원
6	planet	명 행성	16	player	명 선수	26	club	명 클럽, 동호회
7	floor	명 (건물의) 층	17	rest	명 나머지	27	visitor	명 방문객
8	about	전 약, 대략	18	restroom	명 화장실	28	audition	명 오디션
9	member	명 회원	19	the solar system	태양계	29	patient	명 환자
10	flag	명 깃발	20	City Hall	명 시청	30	cancer	명 암

UNIT 09 숫자 표현

My birthday is May 5.
제 생일은 5월 5일이에요.

I'm twelve years old.
저는 열 두 살이에요.

I'm in the fifth grade.
저는 5학년이에요.

A 기수와 서수 참고 3권 부록

영어의 숫자 표현에는 개수(하나, 둘, 셋 등)를 나타내는 기수와 순서(첫째, 둘째, 셋째 등)를 나타내는 서수가 있어요. 개수를 셀 때와 순서를 셀 때 숫자를 읽는 법이 다르므로 잘 알아두도록 해요.

기수		서수	
1	one (하나)	1st	first (첫 번째)
2	two (둘)	2nd	second (두 번째)
3	three (셋)	3rd	third (세 번째)
4	four (넷)	4th	fourth (네 번째)
5	five (다섯)	5th	fifth (다섯 번째)
6	six (여섯)	6th	sixth (여섯 번째)
7	seven (일곱)	7th	seventh (일곱 번째)
8	eight (여덟)	8th	eighth (여덟 번째)
9	nine (아홉)	9th	ninth (아홉 번째)
10	ten (열)	10th	tenth (열 번째)
11	eleven (열하나)	11th	eleventh (열한 번째)
12	twelve (열둘)	12th	twelfth (열두 번째)
13	thirteen (열셋)	13th	thirteenth (열세 번째)
20	twenty (스물)	20th	twentieth (스무 번째)
21	twenty-one (스물하나)	21st	twenty-first (스물한 번째)
22	twenty-two (스물둘)	22nd	twenty-second (스물두 번째)
30	thirty (서른)	30th	thirtieth (서른 번째)
100	a[one] hundred (일백)	100th	hundredth (백 번째)
1,000	a thousand (일천)	1,000th	thousandth (천 번째)

1. 서수는 원칙적으로 기수에 -th를 붙인 형태로 써요.
2. 서수 표현 앞에는 보통 the를 써요.
the first grade (1학년)

B 분수 참고 3권 부록

분수의 분자는 기수로, 분모는 서수로 읽어요. 분자가 2 이상이면 분모 뒤에 -s를 붙여요.

$\frac{1}{2}$	a half, one half (이분의 일)	$\frac{1}{3}$	a third, one third (삼분의 일)	$\frac{1}{4}$	a quarter, one fourth (사분의 일)
$\frac{2}{3}$	two thirds (삼분의 이)	$\frac{3}{5}$	three fifths (오분의 삼)	$\frac{5}{8}$	five eighths (팔분의 오)

C 연도 참고 3권 부록

연도는 대개 두 자리씩 끊어서 기수로 읽어요. 단, 1500년처럼 숫자 0 두 개로 끝나는 연도는 '앞 두자리+hundred'로 읽어요. 2000년 이후의 연도는 일반 숫자를 읽을 때처럼 단위(thousand)를 포함시켜서 읽기도 해요.

1835	eighteen thirty-five	2002	two thousand (and) two / twenty oh-two
1909	nineteen oh-nine		
1500	fifteen hundred	2010	two thousand (and) ten / twenty ten

연도를 읽을 때 숫자 사이의 '0'은 zero가 아닌 oh라고 읽어요.

D 날짜 참고 3권 부록

영어로 날짜를 말할 때는 '요일 → 월 → 일 → 연도' 순으로 쓰고 읽어요.
월·요일을 쓸 때는 첫 글자를 반드시 대문자로 써요.

2018년 7월 7일 토요일	Saturday, July 7(th), 2018 / Saturday, July seventh, two thousand (and) eighteen
2018년 11월 28일 수요일	Wednesday, November 28(th), two thousand (and) eighteen / Wednesday, November twenty-eighth, two thousand (and) eighteen

My Grammar Notes

1 기수는 개수를 나타내는 수를 말하고, 서수는 순서를 나타내는 수를 말한다.

2 분수: 분자 → 기수 / 분모 → 서수 (분자가 2 이상이면, 분모+-s) $\frac{2}{3}$ = two ____________

3 연도: 보통 두 자리씩 끊어 읽는다. (1995: ____________ ninety-five)

4 날짜: '____________ - 월 - 일 - ____________' 순으로 쓰고 읽는다.

Warm-Up

A 보기와 같은 관계가 되도록 빈칸에 알맞은 말을 쓰세요. 기수와 서수

보기 4 – four – fourth

1. 3 → three → third
2. 5 → ______ → ______
3. 8 → ______ → ______
4. 9 → ______ → ______
5. 12 → ______ → ______
6. 18 → ______ → ______
7. 22 → ______ → ______
8. 30 → ______ → ______
9. 51 → ______ → ______
10. 43 → ______ → ______

B ( ) 안에서 주어진 분수를 올바르게 읽은 것을 고르세요. 분수

1. $\frac{1}{2}$ (a half / a two)
2. $\frac{1}{3}$ (first three / one third)
3. $\frac{2}{3}$ (two third / two thirds)
4. $\frac{1}{4}$ (one fourth / one fourths)
5. $\frac{3}{5}$ (three fifth / three fifths)
6. $\frac{3}{4}$ (three fours / three fourths)
7. $\frac{5}{6}$ (five sixths / fifth sixs)
8. $\frac{3}{7}$ (three sevenths / third sevenths)
9. $\frac{5}{9}$ (ninth fifths / five ninths)
10. $\frac{9}{11}$ (nine elevenths / nine elevens)

C 알맞은 연도를 찾아 연결하세요. 연도

1. nineteen ninety-nine •	• ⓐ 2015
2. two thousand and one •	• ⓑ 2001
3. sixteen hundred •	• ⓒ 1865
4. two thousand fifteen •	• ⓓ 1600
5. eighteen sixty-five •	• ⓔ 1999
6. two thousand twenty •	• ⓕ 1805
7. eighteen oh five •	• ⓖ 1987
8. nineteen eighty-seven •	• ⓗ 2020

D 우리말을 영어로 바르게 옮긴 것을 고르세요. 날짜

1. 8월 15일 (August 15 / august 15)
2. 12월 10일 (December 10 / december 10)
3. 1920년 2월 5일 (1920, 5 February / February 5, 1920)
4. 2010년 6월 18일 (2010, June 18 / June 18, 2010)
5. 2017년 10월 9일 (October 9, 2017 / 9 October, 2017)
6. 3월 1일 월요일 (March 1, Monday / Monday, March 1)
7. 4월 9일 금요일 (9 April, Friday / Friday, April 9)
8. 7월 24일 화요일 (July 24, Tuesday / Tuesday, July 24)

Practice

A ( ) 안에서 알맞은 것을 고르세요.

1. 두 개의 사과 → (two / the second) apples
2. 3층 → (three / the third) floor
3. 넷째 주 토요일 → (four / the fourth) Saturday
4. 5학년 → (five / the fifth) grade
5. 세 번째 기회 → (three / the third) chance
6. 나의 열세 번째 생일 → my (thirteen / thirteenth) birthday
7. 나는 15살이다. → I'm (fifteen / fifteenth) years old.
8. 오늘은 10월 1일이다. → Today is October (one / first).
9. 우리는 21세기에 살고 있다.
   → We are living in the (twenty-one / twenty-first) century.
10. 나는 키가 150cm이다.
   → I'm (one hundred and fifty / one hundredth and fiftieth) cm tall.

B 분수는 영어로, 영어는 분수로 쓰세요.

1. $\frac{3}{4}$ → three fourths
2. a fifth →
3. $\frac{2}{3}$ →
4. one half →
5. $\frac{3}{5}$ →
6. five ninths →
7. $\frac{1}{3}$ →
8. four sevenths →
9. $\frac{1}{6}$ →
10. a quarter →

C 다음 연도를 영어로 쓰세요.

1. 1999년 nineteen ninety-nine
2. 2055년
3. 2034년
4. 1756년
5. 2002년
6. 2000년
7. 1660년
8. 2012년
9. 1895년
10. 1944년
11. 2009년
12. 1901년
13. 1400년
14. 1888년

D 우리말과 같은 뜻이 되도록 주어진 말을 이용하여 쓰세요.

1. 4월 5일 (April)
→ April 5

2. 5월 22일 (May)
→

3. 2010년 12월 25일 (December)
→

4. 1999년 11월 13일 (November)
→

5. 2018년 9월 4일 (September)
→

6. 2002년 1월 17일 (January)
→

7. 8월 10일 토요일 (August, Saturday)
→

8. 3월 3일 금요일 (March, Friday)
→

9. 2020년 7월 8일 일요일 (July, Sunday)
→

10. 2021년 6월 7일 월요일 (June, Monday)
→

E 우리말과 같은 뜻이 되도록 알맞은 것을 고르세요.

1. 나의 열두 번째 생일
① my twelvth birthday
② my twelfth birthday
③ my twelve birthdays

2. 그 학생들의 3분의 1
① a thirds of the students
② one third of the students
③ one three of the students

3. 바나나 열 개
① ten bananas
② tenth bananas
③ the tenth bananas

4. 22층
① the twenty-two floor
② twenty-two floors
③ the twenty-second floor

5. 두 번째 기회
① two chances
② the two chance
③ the second chance

6. 100년
① one hundred years
② the hundredth year
③ a hundredth years

7. 2016년 5월 13일
① 2016, 13 May
② 2016, May 13
③ May 13, 2016

8. 일 년의 4분의 3
① three four of a year
② three fourth of a year
③ three fourths of a year

9. 첫째 주 일요일
① one Sunday
② Sunday first
③ the first Sunday

10. 7월 4일 목요일
① July 4, Thursday
② Thursday, July 4
③ 4 July, Thursday

11. 21세기 사람들
① people in the twentieth-first century
② people in the twenty-first century
③ people in the twenty-one century

F 주어진 숫자를 기수 또는 서수로 바꿔 써서 문장을 완성하세요. (필요하면 the를 쓰세요.)

1. I have five cats at my house. (5)
2. It's ______ day of middle school. (1)
3. I'm ______ daughter in my family. (3)
4. We must plant trees on ______ of April. (5)
5. There are ______ planets in the solar system. (8)
6. There are ______ players on a soccer team. (11)
7. Tommy works on ______ floor of this building. (7)
8. Mia is in ______ grade in elementary school. (2)
9. I invited ______ friends to my housewarming party. (12)

G 밑줄 친 부분을 바르게 고쳐 쓰세요.

1. He's <u>the two</u> son in his family. → the second
2. I have <u>the third</u> sisters. → ______
3. I ate <u>three fourth</u> of the cake. → ______
4. Jason is <u>seventh</u> years old. → ______
5. Today is <u>2021, April 30th</u>. → ______
6. The festival will be on <u>6 June</u>. → ______
7. Korean banks are usually on the <u>one</u> floor. → ______

Words

middle school 중학교
daughter 딸
plant (나무를) 심다
planet 행성
the solar system 태양계
player 선수
floor (건물의) 층
grade 학년
elementary school 초등학교
housewarming party 집들이

Grammar into Writing

A 우리말과 같은 뜻이 되도록 틀린 부분을 바르게 고쳐 다시 쓰세요.

1. My brother is the twelfth years old.
(내 동생은 열두 살이다.)
→ My brother is twelve years old.

2. Jeff lost three five of the money.
(Jeff는 그 돈의 5분의 3을 잃어버렸다.)
→ ______________________

3. This is my two audition.
(이것은 내 두 번째 오디션이다.)
→ ______________________

4. Minho is one hundred and eighteen centimeters tall.
(민호의 키는 180cm이다.)
→ ______________________

5. Today is 2019, march 7th, wednesday.
(오늘은 2019년 3월 7일 수요일이다.)
→ ______________________

B 우리말과 같은 뜻이 되도록 문장을 완성하세요.

1. 당신은 오늘 100번째 방문객이십니다.
→ You are the one hundredth visitor today.

2. 그 축제는 7월 9일 월요일에 시작할 것이다.
→ The festival will start on ______________________.

3. 야구팀에는 9명의 선수가 있다.

→ A baseball team has ________________ players.

4. 우리 교실은 4층에 있다.

→ Our classroom is on ________________ floor.

5. 너는 피자의 3분의 1을 먹어도 된다.

→ You can have ________________ of the pizza.

6. 너는 그 빵을 45분 동안 구워야 한다.

→ You must bake the bread for ________________ minutes.

7. 5월 8일은 어버이날이다.

→ ________________ is Parents' Day.

8. 오늘은 할머니의 60번째 생신이다.

→ Today is my grandmother's ________________ birthday.

C 다음 글을 읽고, 밑줄 친 부분을 영어로 바꿔 쓰세요.

Invitation

Hello! I want to invite you to our ❶ 스물세 번째 charity event. Please bring clothes, toys, books, and shoes! This event will be ❷ 2020년 2월 20일 토요일. We are going to give ❸ 5분의 3 of the items to nursing homes. We will sell the rest of them and donate the cash. Please come to the ❹ 11층 of City Hall. We'll wait for you there!

↓

❶ twenty-________________ ❷ ________________

❸ ________________ ❹ ________________

Words **audition** 오디션 **visitor** 방문객 **invitation** 초대(장) **invite** 초대하다 **charity** 자선 **event** 행사, 이벤트 **item** 물건, 물품 **nursing home** 양로원 **rest** 나머지 **donate** 기부하다 **cash** 현금 **City Hall** 시청

Wrap-Up Test

1. 기수와 서수가 잘못 짝지어진 것을 고르세요.

① one – first

② two – second

③ twelve – twelvth

④ twenty – twentieth

⑤ one hundred – one hundredth

2. 우리말을 영어로 바르게 옮긴 것을 고르세요.

① 3분의 1 – a fourth

② 3분의 2 – two third

③ 4분의 3 – four thirds

④ 5분의 2 – two fifths

⑤ 9분의 1 – first ninth

3. 연도를 영어로 바르게 읽은 것을 고르세요.

① 1200 – one two hundred

② 1650 – sixty fifteen

③ 2003 – two hundred three

④ 2009 – two thousand and ninth

⑤ 2031 – two thousand thirty-one

[4-5] 빈칸에 알맞은 말이 바르게 짝지어진 것을 고르세요.

4.

- A dog has __________ legs.
- She is the __________ member of the club.
- I like the __________ song of this album.

① four – seventh – ninth

② four – seventh – nine

③ four – seven – nine

④ fourth – seven – ninth

⑤ fourth – seventh – ninth

5.

- __________ question is easy.
- There are __________ colors on the flag.
- This is the director's __________ movie.

① Two – three – eleventh

② Second – third – eleven

③ The two – third – eleven

④ The second – three – eleven

⑤ The second – three – eleventh

Words **member** 회원 **club** 클럽, 동호회 **album** 앨범, 음반 **question** 질문 **flag** 깃발 **director** 감독

[6-7] 우리말과 영어가 잘못 짝지어진 것을 고르세요.

6.

① 5월 1일 → May 1st

② 열 번째 행성 → ten planet

③ 7층 → the seventh floor

④ 5학년 → the fifth grade

⑤ 내 8번째 생일 → my eighth birthday

7.

① 오늘은 10일입니다.
→ Today is the 10th.

② 그는 나의 세 번째 남동생입니다.
→ He is my third brother.

③ 우리는 책 20권이 있어요.
→ We have twenty books.

④ 그는 30살입니다.
→ He is thirtieth years old.

⑤ 그녀는 반에서 2등입니다.
→ She is the second in her class.

8. 우리말과 같은 뜻이 되도록 주어진 단어를 바르게 배열한 것을 고르세요.

오늘은 2012년 4월 2일 일요일이다. Today is (2012, April, 2nd, Sunday)

① Today is 2012, April 2nd, Sunday.

② Today is Sunday, April 2nd, 2012.

③ Today is Sunday, 2012, April 2nd.

④ Today is 2012, Sunday, 2nd April.

⑤ Today is 2012, Sunday, April 2nd.

9. 틀린 문장을 고르세요.

① There are twenty students.

② The restroom is on the sixth floor.

③ A thirds of the apples are rotten.

④ December 24 is Christmas Eve.

⑤ There are seven days in a week.

[10-11] 우리말과 같은 뜻이 되도록 빈칸에 알맞은 말을 쓰세요.

10.

I'm ________ ________ son in my family. (나는 우리 가족 중에서 둘째 아들이다.)

Words **restroom** 화장실 **rotten** 썩은 **eve** 전날, 전야

11.

About _________ _________ of cancer patients at this hospital survive.
(이 병원에 있는 암 환자들의 약 2분의 1이 살아남는다.)

12. **대화가 어색한 것을 고르세요.**

① A: When is your birthday?
B: February 18.

② A: How old are you?
B: I'm thirteen years old.

③ A: How long is the play?
B: It's the second hours long.

④ A: Where is the Chinese restaurant?
B: It's on the eighth floor.

⑤ A: What grade are you in?
B: I am in the third grade.

13. **틀린 부분을 찾아 바르게 고쳐 쓰세요. (2개)**

We have thousandth guests. He is our hundred guest.

→ ______________________________

____

[14-15] 다음 표를 보고, 물음에 답하세요.

Winter English Camp

When: January 21 – 27

Where: 4th – 5th floor of the Student Center

Participants: 33 people (3 teachers and 30 students)

14. **( ) 안에서 알맞은 말을 고르세요.**

(1) January 21 is the (one / first) day of the Winter English Camp.

(2) (An eleven / An eleventh) of the participants will be teachers.

(3) They will use (two / second) floors for Winter English Camp.

서술형

15. **질문에 대한 대답을 주어진 단어를 이용하여 쓰세요.**

A: How long will Winter English Camp last?

B: It will last _________ _________. (day)

Words **about** 약, 대략 **cancer** 암 **patient** 환자 **survive** 살아남다 **play** 연극 **guest** 손님 **participant** 참가자 **last** 지속되다

UNIT 10

문장의 형태

Vocab Check! 이번 과에서 배울 단어의 뜻을 확인하고, 모르는 단어에 체크 표시하세요.

1	postcard	명 엽서	11	snowman	명 눈사람	21	war	명 전쟁
2	sausage	명 소시지	12	voice	명 목소리	22	clothes	명 옷
3	millions of	수백만의	13	science	명 과학	23	village	명 마을
4	comfortable	형 편안한	14	salt	명 소금	24	calm	형 잔잔한
5	wonderful	형 멋진	15	perfume	명 향수	25	noise	명 소음
6	bored	형 지루해하는	16	ring	명 반지	26	sour	형 신맛이 나는
7	peace	명 평화	17	invent	동 발명하다	27	foreigner	명 외국인
8	expensive	형 비싼	18	cap	명 모자	28	soap	명 비누
9	German	명 독일어	19	big hit	대성공	29	nickname	명 별명
10	cereal	명 시리얼	20	cafeteria	명 구내식당	30	sleepy	형 졸린

UNIT 10 문장의 형태

I baked some cookies for a Halloween party.
나는 핼러윈 파티를 위해 쿠키를 조금 구웠어요.

The cookies taste good. They smell sweet.
그 쿠키들은 맛있어요. 그것들은 달콤한 냄새가 나요.

I will give my friends the cookies at the party.
나는 파티에서 내 친구들에게 그 쿠키를 줄 거예요.

A 주어+동사+형용사 2권 Unit 05

다음 동사 뒤에는 형용사가 와요.

주어	+	look (보이다) smell (냄새가 나다) feel (느낌이 들다)	sound (들리다) taste (맛이 나다)	+	형용사 (~한, ~하게)

The puppy **looks cute**.

Lemons **taste sour**.

The potato pizza **smells good**.

She **feels** very **tired**.

B 주어+동사+명사

다음 동사 뒤에는 동작의 대상이 되는 명사 또는 대명사를 써요.

동사 뒤에 쓰는 대명사는 항상 목적격으로 써요.

주어	+	like (좋아하다) want (원하다) eat (먹다)	have (가지다) change (바꾸다) believe (믿다)	+	대명사 / 명사 (~을)

My friends **like** <u>me</u>. (대명사)

He **wants** <u>a new bike</u>. (명사)

I **eat** <u>pancakes</u> every morning. (명사)

She **has** <u>an alarm clock</u>. (명사)

We **changed** <u>our plans</u>. (명사)

I don't **believe** <u>you</u>. (대명사)

C 주어+동사+(대)명사+명사

'~해주다'의 의미를 갖는 동사들은 대체로 뒤에 두 개의 명사가 필요해요.
주로 첫 번째 명사로 사람을, 두 번째 명사로 사물을 써요.

give (주다) **tell** (말해주다) **make** (만들어주다) **send** (보내주다)	**show** (보여주다) **buy** (사주다) **lend** (빌려주다) **teach** (가르치다)	+	(대)명사 (~에게)	+	명사 (~을)

My boyfriend **gave** me a present.
(me: 대명사, a present: 명사)

He **showed** us his album.
(us: 대명사, his album: 명사)

My sister **told** me her secrets.

Ally's father **bought** her new shoes.

David will **make** you a birthday cake.

Could you **lend** them some money?

Will you **send** me the report by e-mail?

My father **taught** us American history.

Mini Grammar

1. 목적어(~을)에 해당하는 두 번째 명사 자리에는 대명사를 쓸 수 없어요.
He gave me **a letter**. (O) (그는 나에게 편지를 줬어요.)
He gave me **it**. (X) (그는 나에게 그것을 줬어요.)

2. 위의 동사들 뒤에 명사 하나만 써서 문장을 만들 수도 있어요.
She **bought** a bike. (그녀는 자전거를 샀어요.)
Mr. Brown **teaches** English. (Brown 선생님은 영어를 가르쳐요.)

My Grammar Notes

1 look, sound, smell, taste, feel과 같은 동사는 '주어+동사+__________'의 형태로 쓰인다.

2 eat, like, want와 같은 동사는 '주어+동사+__________'의 형태로 쓰인다.

3 give, show, tell, buy와 같은 동사는 '주어+동사+(대)명사+명사'의 형태로 쓰인다.
이때 앞의 (대)명사는 '__________'의 의미를, 뒤의 명사는 '~을'의 의미를 가진다.

Warm-Up

A 다음 문장의 주어에는 O, 동사에는 △, 주어가 아닌 (대)명사에는 □, 형용사에는 밑줄을 그으세요. 그리고 문장의 형태를 쓰세요. 문장의 형태

1. We feel good. → 주어 + 동사 + 형용사
2. He has a car. → ___ + ___ + ___
3. She likes pizza. → ___ + ___ + ___
4. It sounds fun. → ___ + ___ + ___
5. I gave him chocolate. → ___ + ___ + ___ + ___
6. I bought Jenny a ring. → ___ + ___ + ___ + ___
7. The soup tastes bad. → ___ + ___ + ___
8. They took a taxi. → ___ + ___ + ___

Words

ring 반지
soup 수프
bored 지루해하는
sleepy 졸린
voice 목소리
lotion 로션
waffle 와플
earth 지구
fresh 신선한; 상쾌한

B 영어와 우리말 뜻을 바르게 연결하세요. 동사+형용사

1. You look bored. • • ⓐ 지구는 아름답다.
2. She feels sleepy. • • ⓑ 그녀는 졸리다.
3. His voice sounds nice. • • ⓒ 그 빵은 맛이 좋다.
4. This lotion smells good. • • ⓓ 너는 지루해 보인다.
5. The bread tastes great. • • ⓔ 이 로션은 향이 좋다.
6. The waffle tastes sweet. • • ⓕ 그 와플은 달콤하다.
7. The earth looks beautiful. • • ⓖ 바람이 상쾌하다.
8. The wind feels fresh. • • ⓗ 그의 목소리는 멋지다.

C 우리말과 같은 뜻이 되도록 주어진 말이 들어갈 알맞은 곳을 고르세요.

동사+명사

1. 아이들은 만화책을 좋아한다. (love)
→ Children ① comic books ②.

2. 나는 어제 새 게임을 샀다. (bought)
→ I ① a new game ② yesterday.

3. 우리는 교실에서 컴퓨터를 사용한다. (use)
→ We ① computers ② in the classroom.

4. 그녀는 중학교에서 음악을 가르친다. (music)
→ She ① teaches ② at a middle school.

5. 우리는 두 시간 뒤에 시험을 끝냈다. (the exam)
→ We finished ① in two hours ②.

Words

secret 비밀
scarf 스카프
sweater 스웨터
science 과학
cousin 사촌

D '~에게'에 해당하는 말에는 밑줄을 긋고, '~을'에 해당하는 말에는 O 표시하세요.

동사+(대)명사+명사

1. I sent her an e-mail.
2. Bill told him a secret.
3. He bought his mother a scarf.
4. Mom made my brother a sweater.
5. She gave me a science book.
6. David showed her his pictures.
7. My sister taught me English.
8. Ben sent his cousin a birthday card.

Practice

A ( ) 안에서 알맞은 것을 고르세요.

1. Jenny (looks / tastes) happy.
2. The soap (sounds / smells) really good.
3. We (feel / taste) comfortable at home.
4. The singer's voice (tastes / sounds) wonderful.
5. The red roses (feel / smell) sweet.
6. His new coat doesn't (sound / look) warm.
7. The storm (sounds / smells) scary.
8. You (look / smell) tired. You should rest.

B 빈칸에 들어갈 수 없는 것을 고르세요.

1. The bed feels ______. ① soft ② nice ③ cloud
2. The song sounds ______. ① great ② noise ③ calm
3. The juice tastes ______. ① sweet ② sour ③ drink
4. Your lotion smells ______. ① good ② fruit ③ bad
5. These apples look ______. ① fresh ② tasty ③ balls
6. The spaghetti tastes ______. ① sugar ② salty ③ spicy
7. These flowers smell ______. ① great ② nice ③ perfume

Words

soap 비누
comfortable 편안한
wonderful 멋진
rose 장미
warm 따뜻한
storm 폭풍
scary 무서운
tired 피곤한
rest 쉬다
soft 부드러운
noise 소음
calm 잔잔한
sour 신맛이 나는
salty 짠맛이 나는
spicy 매운, 양념 맛이 강한
perfume 향수

C 우리말과 같은 뜻이 되도록 주어진 말을 바르게 배열하세요. 필요하면 형태를 바꾸세요.

Words
mystery novel 추리소설
cafeteria 구내식당
documentary 다큐멘터리, 기록물
war 전쟁

1. 나는 매일 수학을 공부한다. (math / study / I)
→ I study math every day.

2. Jane은 매일 밤 추리소설을 읽는다. (Jane / a mystery novel / read)
→ ______________ every night.

3. 우리는 하루에 세 번 이를 닦는다. (our teeth / we / brush)
→ ______________ three times a day.

4. 그들은 구내식당에서 점심을 먹었다. (ate / lunch / they)
→ ______________ in the cafeteria.

5. 그녀는 오늘 버스를 타지 않았다. (she / the bus / didn't / take)
→ ______________ today.

6. Mina는 이번 주말에 우리를 방문할 것이다. (will / Mina / us / visit)
→ ______________ this weekend.

7. Lucas는 일요일마다 농구를 한다. (play / Lucas / basketball)
→ ______________ every Sunday.

8. 그는 내일 다큐멘터리를 볼 것이다. (he / watch / documentary / will)
→ ______________ tomorrow.

9. 많은 사람들이 그 전쟁을 기억한다. (remember / the war / many people)
→ ______________

D ( ) 안의 말을 알맞은 형태로 쓰세요.

1. My father bought (I) a bike. → me
2. Nell made (he) a bouquet. →
3. Paul sent (she) flowers. →
4. I will tell (you) the story. →
5. I showed (they) my home page. →
6. Mom gave (we) some money. →
7. He lent (my sister) his textbook. →
8. Mr. Kim teaches (his students) Chinese. →

Words

bouquet 부케, 꽃다발
home page 홈페이지
lend 빌려주다 (과거형 **lent**)
textbook 교과서

E 주어진 말이 들어갈 알맞은 위치를 고르세요.

1. Jane — I ① made ② a cake ③.
2. lunch — I ① bought ② my friend ③.
3. the baby — We ① gave ② some milk ③.
4. her — Billy ① told ② a sad story ③ yesterday.
5. English — She ① teaches ② children ③.
6. him — Did you ① send ② a love letter ③?
7. lend — I will ① you ② my new dress ③.
8. me — He didn't ① show ② his old album to ③.

F 밑줄 친 부분을 바르게 고쳐 쓰세요.

1. The village looks peace. → looks peaceful
2. I sleepy feel now. →
3. I cereal ate this morning. →
4. She a new watch wants. →
5. Danny told the secret me. →
6. That funny sounds! →
7. Henry bought I a hamburger. →
8. I my mom made a Christmas card. →

Words

village 마을
peace 평화
cereal 시리얼
practice 연습하다
foreigner 외국인

G 주어진 말을 바르게 배열하여 문장을 완성하세요.

1. (great / smells / this coffee)
   → This coffee smells great.
2. (the actor's / voice / wonderful / sounds)
   →
3. (every day / practice / the guitar / I)
   →
4. (Ms. Lee / Korean / teaches / foreigners)
   →
5. (showed / her diary / Jennifer / me)
   →

Grammar into Writing

A **우리말과 같은 뜻이 되도록 보기의 동사를 이용하여 문장을 완성하세요.**

보기 have give look change lend feel

1. 나는 지루하다. (bored)

→ I feel bored.

2. 그녀는 건강해 보인다. (healthy)

→ ____________________

3. 그녀는 마음을 바꾸지 않았다. (her mind)

→ ____________________

4. 나는 좋은 생각이 있어. (a good idea)

→ ____________________

5. 그는 나에게 그의 신발을 빌려주었다. (his shoes)

→ ____________________

6. 우리는 그녀에게 콘서트 티켓을 주었다. (a concert ticket)

→ ____________________

B **우리말과 같은 뜻이 되도록 주어진 말을 이용하여 문장을 완성하세요.**

1. 1) 지용이는 영어를 잘 말한다. (speak)

→ Jiyong speaks English well.

2) 나의 삼촌은 독일어를 잘 말한다. (my uncle, German)

→ My uncle speaks German well.

2. 1) 나는 그에게 편지를 보냈다. (send)

→ I ___________ ___________ a letter.

2) 그는 나에게 문자 메시지를 보냈다. (text messages)

→ ____

3. 1) 엄마는 새 가방을 사셨다. (buy)

→ My mom ___________ a new bag.

2) 엄마는 나에게 새 자전거를 사주셨다. (bicycle)

→ ____

4. 1) 우리는 크리스마스트리를 만들었다. (make)

→ We ___________ a Christmas tree.

2) 그는 우리에게 커다란 눈사람을 만들어주었다. (a big snowman)

→ ____

C 다음 글을 읽고, 밑줄 친 부분을 바르게 고쳐 쓰세요.

I love cotton candy. It looks like a cloud. It ❶ feels softly. It tastes sweet. Two young men ❷ this invented. In 1904, the young men ❸ showed cotton candy people at a festival. It was a big hit. The sweets ❹ made millions of dollars them!

↓

❶ feels soft

❷ ___________________

❸ ___________________

❹ ___________________

Words **German** 독일어 **text message** 문자 메시지 **snowman** 눈사람 **cotton candy** 솜사탕 **cloud** 구름 **invent** 발명하다 **big hit** 대성공 **sweet** 사탕, 단 것 **millions of** 수백만의

Wrap-Up Test

1. **him이 들어갈 알맞은 위치를 고르세요.**

I ① will ② send ③ a postcard ④ later ⑤.

2. **빈칸에 알맞은 말을 고르세요.**

Did Andy lend _______ a digital camera?

① we
② his
③ hers
④ you
⑤ their

3. **빈칸에 공통으로 알맞은 것을 고르세요.**

- Jihun will _______ a new pair of pants.
- Mom didn't _______ me a new cap.

① have
② want
③ buy
④ taste
⑤ like

[4-5] 빈칸에 들어갈 수 없는 것을 고르세요.

4.

Kate _________ happy today.

① is
② feels
③ has
④ looks
⑤ was

5.

The woman _________ her son the cake.

① showed
② bought
③ made
④ gave
⑤ tasted

Words **postcard** 엽서 **digital camera** 디지털 카메라 **cap** 모자

6. 우리말을 영어로 바르게 옮긴 것을 고르세요.

나는 Ally에게 내 별명을 말해주었다.

① I told Ally.

② I told my nickname.

③ I told my nickname Ally.

④ I told Ally my nickname.

⑤ I tell to Ally my nickname.

7. 빈칸에 알맞은 말이 바르게 짝지어진 것을 고르세요.

- We ________ too tired now.
- I ________ curry this morning.
- Dad ________ me a new cell phone yesterday.

① are – tasted – wanted

② have – smelled – told

③ do – had – showed

④ feel – ate – bought

⑤ look – made – believed

8. 문장의 형태가 다른 하나를 고르세요.

① Sujin lent me her textbook.

② I bought Steve some books.

③ Jennifer made a big apple pie.

④ Ted showed me his diary.

⑤ His uncle taught us Chinese.

9. 올바른 문장을 고르세요.

① This food tastes salt.

② My friend gave me it.

③ Emily helped her parents.

④ The old man looks happily.

⑤ Jim showed the picture her.

10. 틀린 문장을 고르세요.

① They ate steak for lunch.

② This coffee smells good.

③ He gave me some chocolate.

④ Mom made sandwiches us.

⑤ Emma changed her hairstyle.

Words
nickname 별명 **curry** 카레 **salt** 소금 **happily** 행복하게 **steak** 스테이크
hairstyle 머리 모양

11. 영어와 우리말이 잘못 짝지어진 것을 고르세요.

① She looks pretty.
- 그녀는 예뻐 보여.

② This sausage tastes good.
- 이 소시지는 맛있어.

③ The song sounds gloomy.
- 그 노래는 우울하게 들려.

④ Your clothes smell bad.
- 네 옷은 안 어울려.

⑤ My brother feels sleepy.
- 내 남동생은 졸려.

12. 우리말과 같은 뜻이 되도록 빈칸에 알맞은 말을 쓰세요.

너의 새 노트북은 비싸 보여.

→ Your new laptop ________ expensive.

서술형

13. 틀린 부분을 찾아 바르게 고쳐 쓰세요.

Will she tell the story her friends?

→ ____________________________

____

서술형

14. 우리말과 같은 뜻이 되도록 주어진 말을 바르게 배열하세요.

산타클로스는 그 아이들에게 많은 선물을 주었다.
(the children / gave / a lot of presents)

→ Santa Claus ____________________________

____________________________.

서술형

15. 주어진 말을 바르게 배열하여 문장을 완성하세요.

(every day / a letter / the boy / writes)

→ ____________________________

____

Words **sausage** 소시지 **gloomy** 우울한 **clothes** 옷 **laptop** 노트북 컴퓨터 **expensive** 비싼

부록

1 기수와 서수
2 숫자 읽기
3 날짜 표현
4 계절과 날씨
5 시간 표현

1 기수와 서수

기수 (일, 이, 삼, 사 …)		서수 (첫째, 둘째, 셋째, 넷째 …)	
1	one	1st	first
2	two	2nd	second
3	three	3rd	third
4	four	4th	fourth
5	five	5th	fifth
6	six	6th	sixth
7	seven	7th	seventh
8	eight	8th	eighth
9	nine	9th	ninth
10	ten	10th	tenth
11	eleven	11th	eleventh
12	twelve	12th	twelfth
13	thirteen	13th	thirteenth
14	fourteen	14th	fourteenth
15	fifteen	15th	fifteenth
16	sixteen	16th	sixteenth
17	seventeen	17th	seventeenth
18	eighteen	18th	eighteenth
19	nineteen	19th	nineteenth
20	twenty	20th	twentieth
21	twenty-one	21st	twenty-first
22	twenty-two	22nd	twenty-second
23	twenty-three	23rd	twenty-third
24	twenty-four	24th	twenty-fourth
25	twenty-five	25th	twenty-fifth
26	twenty-six	26th	twenty-sixth
27	twenty-seven	27th	twenty-seventh

28	twenty-eight	28th	twenty-eighth
29	twenty-nine	29th	twenty-ninth
30	thirty	30th	thirtieth
40	forty	40th	fortieth
50	fifty	50th	fiftieth
60	sixty	60th	sixtieth
70	seventy	70th	seventieth
80	eighty	80th	eightieth
90	ninety	90th	ninetieth
100	a hundred, one hundred	100th	hundredth
1,000	a thousand	1,000th	thousandth
10,000	ten thousand	10,000th	ten thousandth

2 숫자 읽기

일반 숫자 세 자리씩 끊어 읽는다.

214	two hundred and fourteen
13,526	thirteen thousand five hundred (and) twenty-six

전화번호 한 자리씩 읽는다. 0은 zero 또는 o[oh]로 읽고, 같은 숫자가 연달아 나오면 double을 쓴다.

205-7183	two zero[oh] five, seven one eight three
2014-3551	two zero[oh] one four, three double five one

금액

$7.25	seven dollars (and) twenty-five (cents)
$20.30	twenty dollars (and) thirty (cents)

소수 소수점은 point로 읽고, 소수점 이하는 한 자리씩 읽는다.

3.25	three point two five
11.78	eleven point seven eight

분수 분자는 기수, 분모는 서수로 읽으며, 분자를 먼저 읽고 분모를 읽는다.
분자가 2 이상이면 분모 뒤에 -s를 붙인다.

$\frac{1}{2}$	a half, one half	$\frac{1}{3}$	a third, one third
$\frac{2}{5}$	two fifths	$2\frac{2}{3}$	two and two thirds

사칙연산

1+1 = 2	one plus one equals two, one and one are[is, makes] two
8-3 = 5	eight minus three equals[is] five, three from eight leaves five
5×4 = 20	five multiplied by four equals[is] twenty, five times four is twenty
10÷2 = 5	ten divided by two equals five

3 날짜 표현

연도 보통 두 자리씩 끊어 읽는다.

1979	nineteen seventy-nine
2010	twenty ten / two thousand (and) ten
2009	two thousand (and) nine / twenty oh-nine

날짜 표기 날짜는 '요일 - 월 - 일 - 연도' 순으로 쓴다.
일(日)은 기수나 서수 모두로 나타낼 수 있다.

June 5, 1993	June (the) fifth, nineteen ninety-three (1993년 6월 5일)
August 15th, 2001	August (the) fifteenth, two thousand one (2001년 8월 15일)
Monday, May 10th, 2010	Monday, May tenth, twenty ten (2010년 5월 10일, 월요일)

월(月)

January	1월	February	2월
March	3월	April	4월
May	5월	June	6월
July	7월	August	8월
September	9월	October	10월
November	11월	December	12월

요일

Monday	월요일	Tuesday	화요일
Wednesday	수요일	Thursday	목요일
Friday	금요일	Saturday	토요일
Sunday	일요일		

4 계절과 날씨

사계절

spring	봄	summer	여름	autumn / fall	가을	winter	겨울

날씨를 나타내는 말

sunny / fine / nice	맑은, 화창한	bad	나쁜, 궂은
hot	더운	warm	따뜻한
cold	추운	cool	시원한
chilly	쌀쌀한	windy	바람이 많이 부는
cloudy	구름 낀, 흐린	foggy	안개 낀
dry	건조한	humid	습한
rainy	비가 많이 내리는	snowy	눈이 많이 내리는

5 시간 표현

시간과 분을 순서대로 읽는다.
o'clock은 '시'에만 사용하며 뒤에 '분'이 붙으면 o'clock을 쓰지 않는다.

5:00	five (o'clock)	6:20	six twenty

to / before(~분 전), past / after(~분 후)를 이용해서 나타내기도 한다.
to, before, past, after를 쓸 때, 15분은 주로 a quarter, 30분은 주로 half를 사용한다.

7:15	seven fifteen / a quarter past[after] seven
9:30	nine thirty / half past[after] nine
10:45	ten forty-five / a quarter to[before] eleven

지은이

NE능률 영어교육연구소

NE능률 영어교육연구소는 혁신적이며 효율적인 영어 교재를 개발하고
영어 학습의 질을 한 단계 높이고자 노력하는 NE능률의 연구조직입니다.

Grammar Bean 3

펴 낸 이 주민홍
펴 낸 곳 서울특별시 마포구 월드컵북로 396(상암동) 누리꿈스퀘어 비즈니스타워 10층
㈜NE능률 (우편번호 03925)
펴 낸 날 2019년 1월 5일 개정판 제1쇄 발행
2024년 6월 15일 제11쇄
전 화 02 2014 7114
팩 스 02 3142 0356
홈페이지 www.neungyule.com
등록번호 제1-68호
I S B N 979-11-253-2487-4 63740
정 가 12,000원

NE 능률

고객센터

교재 내용 문의 : contact.nebooks.co.kr (별도의 가입 절차 없이 작성 가능)
제품 구매, 교환, 불량, 반품 문의 : 02-2014-7114
☎ 전화문의는 본사 업무시간 중에만 가능합니다.

NE능률 교재 MAP

문법 구문

아래 교재 MAP을 참고하여 본인의 현재 혹은 목표 수준에 따라 교재를 선택하세요.
NE능률 교재들과 함께 영어실력을 쑥쑥~ 올려보세요!
MP3 등 교재 부가 학습 서비스 및 자세한 교재 정보는 www.nebooks.co.kr 에서 확인하세요.

초1-2

초3
- 그래머버디 1
- 초등영어 문법이 된다 Starter 1

초3-4
- 그래머버디 2
- 초등영어 문법이 된다 Starter 2
- 초등 Grammar Inside 1
- 초등 Grammar Inside 2

초4-5
- 그래머버디 3
- Grammar Bean 1
- Grammar Bean 2
- 초등영어 문법이 된다 1
- 초등 Grammar Inside 3
- 초등 Grammar Inside 4

초5-6
- Grammar Bean 3
- Grammar Bean 4
- 초등영어 문법이 된다 2
- 초등 Grammar Inside 5
- 초등 Grammar Inside 6

초6-예비중
- 능률중학영어 예비중
- Grammar Inside Starter
- 원리를 더한 영문법 STARTER

중1
- 능률중학영어 중1
- Grammar Zone 입문편
- Grammar Zone 워크북 입문편
- 1316 Grammar 1
- 문제로 마스터하는 중학영문법 1
- Grammar Inside 1
- 열중 16강 문법 1
- 쓰기로 마스터하는 중학서술형 1학년
- 중학 천문장 1

중1-2
- 능률중학영어 중2
- 1316 Grammar 2
- 문제로 마스터하는 중학영문법 2
- Grammar Inside 2
- 열중 16강 문법 2
- 원리를 더한 영문법 1
- 중학영문법 총정리 모의고사 1
- 중학 천문장 2

중2-3
- Grammar Zone 기초편
- Grammar Zone 워크북 기초편
- 1316 Grammar 3
- 원리를 더한 영문법 2
- 중학영문법 총정리 모의고사 2
- 쓰기로 마스터하는 중학서술형 2학년
- 중학 천문장 3

중3
- 능률중학영어 중3
- 문제로 마스터하는 중학영문법 3
- Grammar Inside 3
- 열중 16강 문법 3
- 중학영문법 총정리 모의고사 3
- 쓰기로 마스터하는 중학서술형 3학년

예비고-고1
- 문제로 마스터하는 고등영문법
- 올클 수능 어법 start
- 천문장 입문

고1
- Grammar Zone 기본편 1
- Grammar Zone 워크북 기본편 1
- Grammar Zone 기본편 2
- Grammar Zone 워크북 기본편 2
- 필히 통하는 고등 영문법 기본편
- 필히 통하는 고등 서술형 기본편
- 천문장 기본

고1-2
- 필히 통하는 고등 영문법 실력편
- 필히 통하는 고등 서술형 실전편
- TEPS BY STEP G+R Basic

고2-3
- Grammar Zone 종합편
- Grammar Zone 워크북 종합편
- 올클 수능 어법 완성
- 천문장 완성

고3

수능 이상/ 토플 80-89 · 텝스 600-699점
- TEPS BY STEP G+R 1

수능 이상/ 토플 90-99 · 텝스 700-799점
- TEPS BY STEP G+R 2

수능 이상/ 토플 100 · 텝스 800점 이상
- TEPS BY STEP G+R 3

NE 능률

GRAMMAR BEAN

그래머빈

3 Workbook

GRAMMAR BEAN

Workbook 3

CONTENTS

3권

UNIT 01 will, be going to

A will을 이용하여 미래를 나타내는 문장으로 바꿔 쓰세요.

1 I bought a new cell phone.

→ ______________________________ tomorrow.

2 We painted the door last weekend.

→ ______________________________ this weekend.

3 I sent an e-mail this morning.

→ ______________________________ next week.

4 She does yoga every day.

→ ______________________________ this evening.

5 He took many pictures.

→ ______________________________ tomorrow.

B be going to를 이용하여 미래를 나타내는 문장으로 바꿔 쓰세요.

1 Ann sold her car.

→ ______________________________ next week.

2 They went to the library yesterday.

→ ______________________________ this afternoon.

3 She called her father last night.

→ ______________________________ soon.

4 I studied math yesterday.

→ ______________________________ today.

Words **paint** 페인트 칠하다 **send** 보내다 **take a picture** 사진을 찍다 **sell** 팔다 (과거형 **sold**)

C 우리말과 같은 뜻이 되도록 주어진 말을 이용하여 문장을 완성하세요.

1 나는 초콜릿 쿠키를 만들 것이다. (be going to, make)

→ I ______________________ chocolate cookies.

2 그는 10분 후에 돌아 올 것이다. (will, come)

→ He ______________________ back in 10 minutes.

3 그녀는 한복을 입을 것이다. (be going to, wear)

→ She ______________________ a *hanbok*.

4 너는 나와 함께 그곳에 있을 것이다. (will, be)

→ You ______________________ there with me.

5 그들은 축구를 할 것이다. (be going to, play)

→ They ______________________ soccer.

D 밑줄 친 부분을 바르게 고쳐 쓰세요.

1 I'm <u>going buy</u> eggs tomorrow. → ____________________

2 She will <u>sang</u> this evening. → ____________________

3 You're going to <u>are</u> okay. → ____________________

4 He <u>call</u> you tomorrow morning. → ____________________

5 Mom will <u>turns off</u> the radio. → ____________________

6 He will <u>eats</u> out tonight. → ____________________

7 She <u>going to</u> go shopping. → ____________________

Words **come back** 돌아오다 **egg** 달걀 **turn off** (전원을) 끄다 **tonight** 오늘 밤에

UNIT 02 미래시제의 부정문과 의문문

A 지시에 따라 부정문 또는 의문문으로 바꿔 쓰세요.

1 She will arrive on time.
부정문: ______________________ on time.

2 We will see Ally tonight.
의문문: ______________________ tonight?

3 The store will close soon.
의문문: ______________________ soon?

4 He will eat a hamburger for lunch.
부정문: ______________________ for lunch.

5 He is going to study art.
부정문: ______________________ art.

6 She is going to help Jina.
의문문: ______________________ Jina?

7 They are going to sell their house.
부정문: ______________________ their house.

8 She is going to get married next month.
의문문: ______________________ next month?

9 Amy will play the piano at the concert.
부정문: ______________________ at the concert.

10 They are going to study together.
의문문: ______________________ together?

Words **arrive** 도착하다 **on time** 제시간에 **store** 상점, 가게 **art** 미술, 예술 **get married** 결혼하다

B 우리말과 같은 뜻이 되도록 주어진 말을 바르게 배열하세요.

1 Jim이 내일 떠나니? (leave / Jim / will / tomorrow)

→ ______________________________

2 너는 방 청소를 할 거니? (going to / you / clean / are / the room)

→ ______________________________

3 전화 좀 받을래? (answer / you / the phone / will)

→ ______________________________

4 그들은 박물관에 갈 거니? (the museum / they / going to / are / visit)

→ ______________________________

5 너희들은 수영하러 갈 거니? (go swimming / you / going to / are)

→ ______________________________

C 우리말과 같은 뜻이 되도록 빈칸에 알맞은 말을 쓰세요.

1 그녀는 그 컴퓨터를 사려고 하니?

→ ________ she ________ ________ buy the computer?

2 Jack은 그 음악을 듣지 않을 것이다.

→ Jack ________ ________ listen to the music.

3 나는 혼자서 그곳에 가지 않겠다.

→ I ________ go there alone.

4 너는 내일 쇼핑을 하러 갈거니?

→ ________ ________ go shopping tomorrow?

Words **leave** 떠나다 **museum** 박물관 **alone** 혼자

UNIT 03 시제 비교

A

(　　) 안에서 알맞은 것을 고르세요.

1 We (go / are going) swimming every weekend.

2 They (have / are having) a good time now.

3 Sujin (goes / is going) to the park this Sunday.

4 I (take / am taking) a walk tomorrow morning.

5 Brian (visits / will visit) his grandmother next week.

6 I (learned / will learn) Chinese last year.

7 William (visited / is going to visit) a museum two weeks ago.

8 We (cleaned / will clean) our classroom tomorrow.

9 Mr. Johnson (ate / is going to eat) lunch with me yesterday.

10 Jun (played / is going to play) baseball next Saturday.

11 They (play / are playing) basketball right now.

12 Julia (met / will meet) her friends last Sunday.

13 Sally (studied / is studying) English now.

14 I (exercise / am exercising) at the gym every day.

15 Daniel (reads / read) a comic book last night.

Words **Chinese** 중국어 **classroom** 교실 **gym** 체육관

B 주어진 단어를 이용하여 대화를 완성하세요.

1 [play] A: ________ you ________ the guitar every day?
B: No, I don't. I ________ it on Sundays.

2 [study] A: ________ you ________ Japanese last year?
B: No, I didn't. I ________ Chinese.

3 [drink] A: ________ Lily ________ kiwi juice right now?
B: Yes, she is.

4 [do] A: ________ you ________ your homework tonight?
B: Yes, I will.

5 [meet] A: ________ Tom ________ his girlfriend tomorrow?
B: No, he isn't. He will meet her next Sunday.

C 밑줄 친 부분이 맞으면 O, 틀리면 바르게 고쳐 쓰세요.

1 She <u>didn't sleep</u> right now. → ____________

2 Last year she <u>will move</u> to New York. → ____________

3 They <u>starts</u> a new project last year. → ____________

4 <u>I'm going</u> shopping next Sunday. → ____________

5 Billy <u>doesn't play</u> a computer game now. → ____________

6 We <u>dance</u> around the campfire last night. → ____________

7 <u>I'm going to study</u> art in France next year. → ____________

8 He <u>doesn't go</u> to bed early on the weekends. → ____________

Words **Japanese** 일본어 **kiwi** 키위 **project** 프로젝트 **campfire** 모닥불

Grammar Test

[1-4] 다음 문장을 보기와 같이 미래시제로 바꾸어 쓰세요.

> [보기] John goes to school at 8 o'clock. (will)
>
> → John will go to school at 8 o'clock.

1 I don't eat chocolate. (be going to)

→ ______________________________

2 Does Jimmy take pictures? (will)

→ ______________________________

3 Do you come home early? (be going to)

→ ______________________________

4 Dorothy shops online. (will)

→ ______________________________

[5-8] 미래시제를 써서 대화를 완성하세요.

5 A: ________ you study French next month?

B: No, I ________.

6 A: ________ your friends going to sing the song?

B: Yes, they ________.

7 A: ________ Tony send the letter next Monday?

B: Yes, he ________.

8 A: Is she going to go to the concert tonight?

B: No, she ________.

Words **early** 일찍 **shop** 쇼핑하다, 사다 **French** 프랑스어 **letter** 편지

[9-14] 주어진 말을 사용하여 문장을 완성하세요.

9 Ms. Johnson ____________ her son yesterday. (call)

10 Her son ____________ math now. (study)

11 He ____________ pizza right now. (eat)

12 She ____________ the train ticket last night. (buy)

13 He ____________ at 6 o'clock every morning. (get up)

14 Kelly ____________ tomorrow morning. (leave)

[15-19] 틀린 부분을 찾아 바르게 고쳐 쓰세요.

15 The actor will shows up at the party tomorrow. ________ → ________

16 Will Anna going to join the drama club? ________ → ________

17 You'll met my boss at the next meeting. ________ → ________

18 My phone doesn't work yesterday. ________ → ________

19 Tina is wait for you right now. ________ → ________

20 빈칸에 알맞은 것을 모두 고르세요. (3개)

Mike and I ________ shopping tomorrow.

① will go ② went

③ are going ④ are going to go

Words

leave 떠나다 **actor** (남자) 배우 **boss** 상사 **meeting** 회의 **work** 일하다; 작동하다
wait for ~를 기다리다

[21-25] **우리말과 같은 뜻이 되도록 주어진 말을 이용하여 문장을 만드세요.**

21 우리는 좋은 시간을 보냈다. (have a good time)

→ ______________________________

22 그는 Jenny의 생일을 잊지 않을 것이다. (will, forget Jenny's birthday)

→ ______________________________

23 우리는 그의 소설을 읽고 있는 중이다. (read his novel)

→ ______________________________

24 그는 아침마다 조깅하러 간다. (go jogging, every morning)

→ ______________________________

25 너는 수영을 배울 거니? (be going to, learn swimming)

→ ______________________________

[26-28] **대화가 어색한 것을 고르세요.**

26

① A: Are you going to visit New York?
B: Yes, I am. I have many friends there.

② A: Are they going to stay at home?
B: No, they aren't. They'll go out.

③ A: Are you going to the library?
B: Yes, I am. I'm going to the concert.

④ A: Are they going to call you?
B: Yes, they are. I'm waiting for their call.

Words **forget** 잊다 **novel** 소설 **visit** 방문하다 **stay** 머무르다 **library** 도서관

27 ① A: Will you join the game?

B: Sure. Let's play together.

② A: Will you wash the dishes?

B: No, I am not. I don't like doing that.

③ A: Are you going to read the newspaper?

B: Yes, I am.

④ A: Are you going to set the table?

B: No, I'm not. I won't do it.

28 ① A: Are you a doctor?

B: No, I'm not. I am a police officer.

② A: Did you read my e-mail?

B: Yes, I did. I'll write back to you soon.

③ A: Are you crying?

B: Yes, I am. I'm reading a sad story.

④ A: Do you like this salad?

B: Yes, I am. I am eating it soon.

29 **밑줄 친 부분의 의미가 다른 하나를 고르세요.**

① Lucy is going to the park.

② Jane is going to go fishing.

③ He is going to meet his friend.

④ She is going to study tonight.

Words **newspaper** 신문 **set the table** 식탁을 차리다 **park** 공원 **go fishing** 낚시하러 가다

UNIT 04 can, must, may

A **우리말과 같은 뜻이 되도록 보기에서 알맞은 조동사를 골라 문장을 완성하세요.**

[보기] must can may

1 나는 지금 당장 집에 가야 한다. (go)
→ I ____________ home right now.

2 나는 바다에서 수영을 할 수 있다. (swim)
→ I ____________ in the sea.

3 너는 사실을 말해야 한다. (tell)
→ You ____________ the truth.

4 너는 그곳에 가도 된다. (go)
→ You ____________ there.

B **두 문장이 같은 뜻이 되도록 빈칸에 알맞은 말을 쓰세요.**

1 Ally can run very fast.
= Ally ________ ________ ________ run very fast.

2 You must keep the secret.
= You ________ ________ keep the secret.

3 You may leave the room.
= You ________ leave the room.

4 They can climb that mountain.
= They ________ ________ ________ climb that mountain.

5 Jenny must see a doctor.
= Jenny ________ ________ see a doctor.

Words **truth** 진실, 사실 **keep a secret** 비밀을 지키다 **climb** 오르다

C

우리말과 같은 뜻이 되도록 주어진 말을 이용하여 문장을 완성하세요.

1 나는 영어를 가르칠 수 있다. (teach English)

→ ______________________________

2 너는 그 책을 읽어야 한다. (read the book)

→ ______________________________

3 너는 사진을 찍어도 된다. (take pictures)

→ ______________________________

4 그녀는 파스타를 만들 수 있다. (make pasta)

→ ______________________________

5 그는 잠시 휴식을 취해야만 한다. (take a break)

→ ______________________________

6 너는 그 콘서트에 가도 된다. (go to the concert)

→ ______________________________

D

밑줄 친 부분을 바르게 고쳐 쓰세요.

1 The boy can speaks Chinese. → ____________

2 They are able to played the flute. → ____________

3 Dan and Ally has to hurry up. → ____________

4 Bill mays answer the phone. → ____________

5 I must cleaned the house. → ____________

6 Lucy is able swim. → ____________

7 She have to stay here. → ____________

Words **take a break** 휴식을 취하다 **flute** (악기) 플루트 **hurry up** 서두르다 **answer** (전화를) 받다

UNIT 05 조동사의 부정문

A 우리말과 같은 뜻이 되도록 (   ) 안에서 알맞은 것을 고르세요.

1 나는 이 문제를 풀 수 없다.
→ I (cannot / may not) solve this problem.

2 너는 여기서 길을 건너면 안 된다.
→ You (don't have to / must not) cross the street here.

3 우리는 우산을 가져갈 필요가 없다.
→ We (don't have to / must not) take umbrellas.

4 너는 이 우유를 마시면 안 된다.
→ You (don't have to / may not) drink this milk.

5 그는 노래를 잘 부르지 못한다.
→ He (may not / isn't able to) sing well.

B 밑줄 친 부분을 바르게 고쳐 쓰세요.

1 You must wear not the sneakers. → ______________

2 He cannot understands me. → ______________

3 You not may use this computer. → ______________

4 She doesn't has to bring the bags. → ______________

5 You mustn't not eat junk food. → ______________

6 I am able not to meet them. → ______________

Words **solve** (문제를) 풀다 **cross** 건너다 **sneakers** 운동화 **bring** 가져오다 **junk food** 정크푸드 (영양가 없는 인스턴트 식품 등)

C 두 문장이 비슷한 뜻이 되도록 (   ) 안에서 알맞은 것을 고르세요.

1 You can't go now. → You (don't have to / may not) go now.

2 I can't jump high. → I (am not able to / must not) jump high.

3 I can't sleep well.
→ I (am not able to / may not) sleep well.

4 You may not stay here.
→ You (aren't able to / can't) stay here.

5 He can't speak Korean.
→ He (isn't able to / may not) speak Korean.

6 You may not eat in the classroom.
→ You (aren't able to / cannot) eat in the classroom.

D 우리말과 같은 뜻이 되도록 주어진 말을 이용하여 문장을 완성하세요.

1 너는 그것에 대해 걱정할 필요가 없다. (have to)
→ You ________________________ worry about it.

2 나는 저 상자들을 들 수 없다. (able to)
→ I ________________________ lift those boxes.

3 그들은 그 운동장을 사용하면 안 된다. (may)
→ They ________________________ use the playground.

4 그는 일본어를 읽지 못한다. (can)
→ He ________________________ read Japanese.

5 도서관에서 소음을 내면 안 된다. (must)
→ You ________________________ make noise in the library.

Words **high** 높이 **lift** 들어 올리다 **playground** 운동장, 놀이터 **make noise** 시끄럽게 하다

UNIT 06 조동사의 의문문

A 우리말과 같은 뜻이 되도록 ( ) 안에서 알맞은 것을 고르세요.

1 제가 여기에 있어도 되나요?
→ (Can / Must) I stay here?

2 제가 설거지를 해야 할까요?
→ (Can I / Do I have to) wash the dishes?

3 그는 피아노를 칠 수 있나요?
→ (Can / Must) he play the piano?

4 이 문제를 풀 수 있나요?
→ (Must you / Are you able to) solve this problem?

5 저를 위해 이것을 해주실 수 있나요?
→ (Do you have to / Can you) do this for me?

6 제가 그녀와 이야기를 해도 될까요?
→ (May I / Do I have to) talk to her?

B 밑줄 친 부분을 바르게 고쳐 쓰세요.

1 Can I <u>asking</u> you a question? → ______
2 Must she <u>finishes</u> this work? → ______
3 <u>Is</u> you able to come? → ______
4 <u>Do</u> the child have to wear jeans? → ______
5 Must I <u>am</u> quiet? → ______
6 <u>Does</u> she able to speak English? → ______

Words **jeans** 청바지 **quiet** 조용한

C 다음 문장을 의문문으로 바꾸고, 질문에 알맞은 대답을 완성하세요.

1 Paul can join the basketball team.

→ ______________________________ – Sorry, _______________.

2 I may play the computer game.

→ ______________________________ – Yes, _______________.

3 Kelly can take this umbrella.

→ ______________________________ – Of course _______________.

4 Ms. Brown can swim fast.

→ ______________________________ – Yes, _______________.

5 They have to take a bus.

→ ______________________________ – No, _______________.

6 I must clean the room now.

→ ______________________________ – No, _______________.

7 They are able to speak French.

→ ______________________________ – Yes, _______________.

8 You are able to do your homework alone.

→ ______________________________ – Yes, _______________.

9 He must call his family first.

→ ______________________________ – No, _______________.

10 She can go outside now.

→ ______________________________ – No, _______________.

Words **alone** 혼자서 **outside** 밖에

Grammar Test

[1-6] 우리말과 같은 뜻이 되도록 주어진 말을 이용하여 문장을 완성하세요.

1 너는 네 친구들과 싸우면 안 된다. (must)

→ You ________________ fight with your friends.

2 너는 영어를 할 수 있니? (can)

→ ________________ you speak English?

3 나는 도서관에 갈 필요가 없다. (have to)

→ I ________________ go to the library.

4 네 전화기를 좀 사용할 수 있을까? (may)

→ ________________ I use your phone?

5 너는 지금 당장 네 숙제를 제출해야 해. (have to)

→ You ________________ hand in your homework right now.

6 나는 수영을 할 수 없어. 물이 무서워. (be able to)

→ I ________________ swim. I'm afraid of water.

[7-12] 밑줄 친 부분을 바르게 고쳐 쓰세요.

7 Jamie can <u>cooks</u> very well. → ________________

8 She <u>have to</u> find the key. → ________________

9 Dan isn't <u>able run</u> 100 m in 10 seconds. → ________________

10 May <u>go I</u> now? → ________________

11 The bird cannot <u>flies</u>. → ________________

12 You must not <u>entered</u> the room. → ________________

Words **hand in** 제출하다 **be afraid of** ~을 두려워하다 **second** (시간의) 초 **enter** 들어가다

[13-19] 대화의 빈칸에 can, may, must 중 알맞은 것을 쓰세요. 필요하면 형태를 바꾸세요.

13 A: ________ I go with you?

B: Sorry, but you can't.

14 A: Did you see my cell phone? I ________ find it.

B: Did you check your bag?

15 A: Can you come to my house?

B: No, I can't. I ________ do my homework.

16 A: ________ I send the file?

B: Oh, you don't have to do that. I already have it.

17 A: My computer doesn't work.

B: Don't worry. You ________ use mine.

18 A: You ________ clean your room now. Mom will come back soon.

B: Okay. I will.

19 A: Can you ride a bike?

B: Yes. I ________ drive a car, too.

[20-22] (   ) 안에서 알맞은 것을 고르세요.

20 You (must not / don't have to) take an umbrella. It'll be sunny today.

21 I (can't / am able to) find my wallet. Maybe I lost it.

22 You (have to / may) hurry up. You have only five minutes.

Words **wallet** 지갑 **lose** 잃어버리다 (과거형 **lost**)

[23-27] 우리말과 같은 뜻이 되도록 주어진 말을 이용하여 문장을 만드세요.

23 너는 걱정할 필요가 없다. (worry)

→ ______________________________

24 너는 낚시를 하러 가도 된다. (go fishing)

→ ______________________________

25 전화를 끊어서는 안 된다. (must, hang up the phone)

→ ______________________________

26 나는 그 영화를 이해할 수 없다. (understand the movie)

→ ______________________________

27 그들은 비밀을 지켜야만 한다. (keep the secret)

→ ______________________________

[28-29] 보기에 밑줄 친 조동사와 같은 의미로 쓰인 것을 고르세요.

28

[보기] You can visit me again.

① I can speak Chinese.

② Can I leave now?

③ I can understand you.

④ I can hear you.

29

[보기] I have to wait for him.

① She can come here.

② May I ask you a question?

③ You must ask me first.

④ You'll be able to sing that song.

Words **worry** 걱정하다 **hang up** 전화를 끊다

30 질문에 대한 대답으로 알맞은 것을 모두 고르세요. (2개)

A: Can you carry my bag for me?

B: ______________________________

① No problem. Give it to me.

② Yes, you can. You can carry heavy bags.

③ Sorry, but I can't. I have to carry my bags.

④ No, I can't. I may carry your bag.

31 틀린 문장을 고르세요.

① Can I take this umbrella?

② You must not hurt others' feelings.

③ He can be able to play the piano.

④ She has to buy the book.

32 짝지어진 문장의 의미가 서로 다른 것을 고르세요.

① You can turn on the TV.
– You may turn on the TV.

② I must take this medicine.
– I have to take this medicine.

③ I can climb that mountain.
– I'm able to climb that mountain.

④ You mustn't make any noise.
– You don't have to make any noise.

Words **carry** 들고 있다 **hurt** 다치게 하다 **feelings** 감정 **medicine** 약

UNIT 07 부사

A 영어와 우리말을 바르게 연결하세요.

1 early •	• ⓐ 슬프게
2 lately •	• ⓑ 일찍
3 well •	• ⓒ 최근에
4 sadly •	• ⓓ 잘
5 really •	• ⓔ 운이 좋게
6 luckily •	• ⓕ 높게
7 high •	• ⓖ 정말로

B A에서 알맞은 부사를 골라 빈칸에 쓰세요. (한 번씩만 쓰세요.)

1 I get up ________ in the morning.

2 She plays the piano very ________.

3 ________, I found my lost bag.

4 The man climbed ________ on the ladder.

5 The movie was ________ interesting.

6 Jessica cried ________ last night.

7 You look tired ________.

Words **lost** 잃어버린 **ladder** 사다리 **interesting** 흥미로운 **cry** 울다

C

(　　) 안에서 알맞은 것을 고르세요.

1 My watch is (slow / slowly).

2 The flowers in the garden are so (beautiful / beautifully).

3 Students solved the math problem (simple / simply).

4 You should be (nice / nicely) to him.

5 Kate touched the cat (soft / softly).

6 She entered the room (quiet / quietly).

7 They lived (happy / happily).

D

우리말과 같은 뜻이 되도록 주어진 말을 이용하여 문장을 완성하세요.

1 비가 세차게 내리고 있다. (hard)

→ It's raining ________.

2 아이들이 운동장에서 즐겁게 놀고 있다. (happy)

→ Children are playing ________ on the playground.

3 그는 천천히 돌아섰다. (slow)

→ He turned around ________.

4 그는 내게 친절하게 대해 주었다. (kind)

→ He treated me ________.

5 Alex는 조용히 그 문을 닫았다. (quiet)

→ Alex closed the door ________.

6 선생님은 그 이유를 명확히 설명했다. (clear)

→ The teacher explained the reason ________.

Words **touch** 만지다 **enter** 들어가다 **treat** 대하다 **clear** 명확한 **explain** 설명하다 **reason** 이유

UNIT 08 빈도부사

A 주어진 빈도부사를 이용하여 문장을 다시 쓰세요.

1 Peter likes singing. (always)

→ ____________________

2 I fight with my brother. (never)

→ ____________________

3 Jack is late for school. (often)

→ ____________________

4 He takes me to the zoo. (sometimes)

→ ____________________

5 They watch TV in the evening. (never)

→ ____________________

6 She goes to dance parties. (often)

→ ____________________

7 I can take a vacation. (sometimes)

→ ____________________

8 People make mistakes. (usually)

→ ____________________

9 He is smiling. (always)

→ ____________________

10 Billy is kind to me. (sometimes)

→ ____________________

Words **fight** 싸우다 **late** 늦은, 지각한 **mistake** 실수

B 다음은 7명의 학생을 대상으로 방과 후 활동을 조사한 내용입니다. 표의 내용과 일치하도록 빈도부사를 이용하여 문장을 완성하세요.

Question	always	often	some-times	never
How often do you go to the library?	Kate	Jinhee, Sehun, Minji	Taehee, Minsu	Sunny
How often do you watch TV?	Sunny	Taehee, Sehun	Jinhee, Minji	Minsu, Kate
How often do you exercise?	Minsu	Minji	Taehee, Sehun	Kate, Jinhee, Sunny

1 Kate studies hard.
She ________ ________ to the library after school.

2 Sunny ________ ________ to the library after school.
She ________ ________ TV.

3 Minsu ________ ________ TV.
He ________ exercises after school.

4 Taehee ________ exercises after school.
He ________ watches TV.

5 Three students ________ exercise.
They don't like to exercise.

6 Taehee and Sehun ________ ________ TV.
They love music programs.

Words **exercise** 운동하다 **after school** 방과 후에

Grammar Test

[1-6] **보기에서 알맞은 부사를 골라 빈칸에 쓰세요.**

[보기] very slowly fortunately loudly suddenly badly

1 I can't hear you. Can you speak ________?

2 The boy doesn't listen to his mom. He acts ________.

3 It's too fast. You must drive ________.

4 ________, we caught the last train.

5 I won't watch that movie again. It's ________ scary.

6 ________, the car hit a tree.

[7-12] **밑줄 친 부분을 바르게 고쳐 쓰세요.**

7 Can you <u>sing good</u>? → ________________

8 I <u>drink sometimes</u> diet cola. → ________________

9 The child doesn't <u>eat good</u>. → ________________

10 The bird can <u>fly fastly</u>. → ________________

11 <u>How do often</u> you exercise? → ________________

12 He worked <u>very hardly</u>. → ________________

Words **act** 행동하다 **scary** 무서운 **hit** 들이받다

[13-18] **보기에서 알맞은 말을 골라 대화를 완성하세요.**

[보기] often quickly quietly easily late early

13 A: How ________ do you go shopping?
B: Every Sunday.

14 A: You look sleepy.
B: I'm tired. I got up ________ this morning.

15 A: Is this an easy question?
B: Yes. You can answer it ________.

16 A: Do you want quick delivery service?
B: Yes. Deliver them ________, please.

17 A: Were you late at the meeting?
B: Yes. I arrived there 10 minutes ________.

18 A: The baby is sleeping.
B: I'll close the door ________.

[19-21] **( ) 안에서 알맞은 것을 고르세요.**

19 I don't like seafood. I (always / never) eat it.

20 (Honest / Honestly), I don't understand him.

21 This song is (amazing / amazingly) beautiful.

Words **delivery** 배송, 배달 **deliver** 배달하다 **arrive** 도착하다 **seafood** 해산물 **honestly** 솔직히 **amazing** 굉장한

[22-26] 우리말과 같은 뜻이 되도록 주어진 말을 이용하여 문장을 만드세요.

22 갑자기 그는 창문을 열었다. (suddenly, open the window)

→ ______________________________

23 그녀는 항상 다른 사람들에 대해 이야기한다. (always, talk about other people)

→ ______________________________

24 운이 좋게도, 나는 택시를 잡았다. (luckily, take a taxi)

→ ______________________________

25 그는 종종 등산을 한다. (often, climb mountains)

→ ______________________________

26 그녀는 결코 운동을 하지 않는다. (never, exercise)

→ ______________________________

[27-28] 빈칸에 들어갈 수 없는 것을 고르세요.

27

I sometimes ______________.

① go to the gym
② study math
③ make cookies
④ will swim

28

He smiled ______________.

① warmly
② brightly
③ strangely
④ happy

Words **warmly** 따뜻하게 **brightly** 밝게 **strangely** 이상하게

29 **질문에 대한 대답으로 알맞은 것을 고르세요.**

A: How often do you go shopping?

B: ______________________________

① Once a week.

② Yes, I do. I like shopping.

③ Honestly, I don't go there.

④ No, I don't. I never go shopping.

30 **틀린 문장을 고르세요.**

① She usually does the dishes.

② He sang the song quiet.

③ I often change my mind.

④ You must listen to me carefully.

31 **대화가 어색한 것을 고르세요.**

① A: Can you go to the concert tonight?

B: Sure. I'll never go to the concert.

② A: Do they often eat out?

B: Yes, they do.

③ A: How often do you ride a bike?

B: Twice a week.

④ A: Do you usually have lunch with Amy?

B: Yes, she is my best friend.

Words **change one's mind** 마음을 바꾸다 **carefully** 주의 깊게 **eat out** 외식하다

UNIT 09 숫자 표현

A 질문에 알맞은 대답을 바르게 연결하세요.

1	How tall are you? •	• ⓐ It's on the 7th floor.
2	When is your birthday? •	• ⓑ For two weeks.
3	How old is your sister? •	• ⓒ June 17.
4	Where is your office? •	• ⓓ She's 14 years old.
5	How long will you stay here? •	• ⓔ I'm 165 cm tall.
6	When will you get married? •	• ⓕ On September 24 next year.

B 주어진 숫자를 알맞은 영어 표현으로 바꿔 쓰세요.

1 We need ____________ copies of this paper. (10)

2 I'll go to Paris on the ____________ of July. (22)

3 I have ____________ sisters and one brother. (3)

4 I am the ____________ child. (1)

5 I waited for you in the library for ____________ minutes. (30)

6 Can you lend me ____________ dollars? (50)

7 I read ____________ books in a year. (12)

8 I'll give you the ____________ chance. (2)

Words **stay** 머물다 **get married** 결혼하다 **copy** 복사물 **lend** 빌려주다 **chance** 기회

C 우리말과 같은 뜻이 되도록 밑줄 친 부분을 바르게 고쳐 쓰세요.

1 그녀는 2개의 히트곡을 작곡했다.
→ She wrote second hit songs. → ______________

2 이것은 내 여섯 번째 일기장이다.
→ This is my six diaries. → ______________

3 그는 가족 중 장남이다.
→ He is one son in his family. → ______________

4 이것은 내 두 번째 차이다.
→ This is my two car. → ______________

5 학생의 3분의 2가 여학생이었다.
→ Two third of the students were women. → ______________

D ( ) 안에서 알맞은 것을 고르세요.

1 She has (three / third) houses.

2 Yesterday was my (ten / tenth) birthday.

3 He ate (three fifth / three fifths) of the cake.

4 We'll meet (two Saturday / the second Saturday) this month.

5 (Half / One second) of the students will be there.

6 I can speak (third / three) languages.

7 The bank is on the (two / second) floor.

8 I read (two thirds / second thirds) of the book.

Words **language** 언어

UNIT 10 문장의 형태

A 우리말과 같은 뜻이 되도록 보기의 단어를 이용하여 문장을 완성하세요.

[보기] taste smell sound look

1 너의 새 헤어스타일은 멋져 보인다. (nice)

→ Your new hairstyle ________ ________.

2 이 케이크는 달콤한 맛이 난다. (sweet)

→ This cake ________ ________.

3 그 새의 노래는 아름답게 들린다. (beautiful)

→ The bird's song ________ ________.

4 그의 방에서 나쁜 냄새가 난다. (bad)

→ His room ________ ________.

B 우리말과 같은 뜻이 되도록 주어진 말을 바르게 배열하세요.

1 Jason은 파란 모자를 썼다. (a / cap / wore / blue / Jason)

→ ________________________________

2 그녀는 큰 우산을 가져갔다. (umbrella / a / took / big / she)

→ ________________________________

3 나는 큰 나무를 그리려고 한다. (tree / going / a / to / I / draw / tall / am)

→ ________________________________

4 그는 커피 한잔을 마셨다. (cup / drank / coffee / he / of / a)

→ ________________________________

Words **sweet** 달콤한 **umbrella** 우산 **draw** 그리다

C 우리말과 같은 뜻이 되도록 보기의 단어를 이용하여 문장을 완성하세요.

[보기] give tell bring lend send teach make buy

1 나는 그에게 강아지를 주었다. (a puppy / him)

→ I ______________________________.

2 아빠는 나에게 새 컴퓨터를 사 주셨다. (me / a new computer)

→ Dad ______________________________.

3 Jennifer는 나에게 그녀의 교과서를 빌려 주었다. (her textbook / me)

→ Jennifer ______________________________.

4 나는 내 여동생에게 재미난 이야기를 말해 주었다. (my sister / a funny story)

→ I ______________________________.

5 Holiday 씨는 나에게 스페인어를 가르쳐 주셨다. (Spanish / me)

→ Mr. Holiday ______________________________.

6 나는 그 아이들에게 모래성을 만들어 주었다. (a sandcastle / the children)

→ I ______________________________.

7 그는 Dan에게 이메일을 보냈다. (Dan / an e-mail)

→ He ______________________________.

8 Daniel은 그의 남동생에게 몇 권의 책을 가져다주었다.
(his brother / some books)

→ Daniel ______________________________.

Words **puppy** 강아지 **textbook** 교과서 **Spanish** 스페인어 **sandcastle** 모래성

Grammar Test

[1-7] **밑줄 친 부분을 보기와 같이 영어로 쓰세요.**

[보기] The store is on the 3rd floor. → third

1 She was born in 2001. → ____________

2 This is the 2nd chance. → ____________

3 I need $\frac{2}{5}$ of that. → ____________

4 My birthday is September 12. → ____________

5 It's the 1st day of the month. → ____________

6 It's my 4th dog. → ____________

7 Today is Thursday, May 30, 2019. → ____________

[8-10] **우리말과 같은 뜻이 되도록 ( ) 안에서 알맞은 것을 고르세요.**

8 그는 티켓의 3분의 2를 샀다.

→ He bought (two threes / two thirds) of the tickets.

9 그녀는 3학년이었다.

→ She was in the (three / third) grade.

10 그 가수는 62번째 그래미 시상식에서 여섯 개의 상을 수상했다.

→ The singer won (six / sixth) awards at the (sixty-two / sixty-second) Grammy Awards.

Words **store** 가게 **floor** 층 **chance** 기회 **award** 상

[11-15] **우리말과 같은 뜻이 되도록 주어진 말을 바르게 배열하세요.**

11 나에게 네 가방을 빌려줄래? (bag / you / me / lend / your / will)

→ ______________________________

12 그녀는 나에게 영어를 가르쳐주었다. (English / she / me / taught)

→ ______________________________

13 Tony는 Julia에게 책을 한 권 주었다. (a book / Tony / Julia / gave)

→ ______________________________

14 나는 피자 세 조각을 먹었다. (pizza / I / of / pieces / three / ate)

→ ______________________________

15 나의 부모님은 나에게 사진 한 장을 보여주셨다.
(a picture / my parents / me / showed)

→ ______________________________

[16-20] **틀린 부분을 찾아 바르게 고쳐 쓰세요.**

16 This coffee tastes well. ________ → ________

17 He made my a chair. ________ → ________

18 I milk drank. ________ → ________

19 The soup smells a sweet. ________ → ________

20 Will you bring ours the umbrella? ________ → ________

Words **lend** 빌려주다 **chair** 의자 **soup** 수프 **bring** 가져오다 **umbrella** 우산

[21-26] **우리말과 같은 뜻이 되도록 주어진 말을 사용하여 문장을 만드세요.**

21 너는 슬퍼 보인다. (sad)

→ ______________________________

22 나는 그녀를 5층에서 만났다. (meet her, on, floor)

→ ______________________________

23 나는 그 빵의 3분의 1을 먹었다. (eat, the bread)

→ ______________________________

24 그는 나에게 그의 운동화를 빌려주었다. (lend, his sneakers)

→ ______________________________

25 그녀는 오렌지 주스 두 잔을 마셨다. (drink, glasses of orange juice)

→ ______________________________

26 Mary는 빨간 드레스 하나를 가지고 있다. (have, a red dress)

→ ______________________________

[27-28] **빈칸에 알맞은 것을 모두 고르세요. (2개)**

27

They bought ____________.

① some flowers

② many beautiful

③ their daughter some flowers

④ many flowers those people

Words **sneakers** 운동화 **daughter** 딸

28 This steak tastes ___________.

① terribly

② is good

③ bad

④ very good

[29-31] 틀린 문장을 고르세요.

29

① I have two hundred dollars in my wallet.

② A half of the children like the movie.

③ My brother told me his secrets.

④ Your plan sounds interestingly.

30

① I saw your two sisters.

② Why were you on the eighth floor?

③ This is the second message from them.

④ He's the three son in his family.

31

① I ate two fifths of the pizza.

② I put third bananas on the table.

③ The village looks peaceful.

④ Danny taught Koreans English.

Words **wallet** 지갑 **secret** 비밀 **plan** 계획 **message** 메시지 **son** 아들 **village** 마을 **peaceful** 평화로운

UNIT 01 will, be going to

A 1 I will buy a new cell phone
2 We will paint the door
3 I will send an e-mail
4 She will do yoga
5 He will take many pictures

B 1 Ann is going to sell her car
2 They are going to go to the library
3 She is going to call her father
4 I am going to study math

C 1 am going to make 2 will come
3 is going to wear 4 will be
5 are going to play

D 1 going to buy 2 sing 3 be
4 will[is going to] call 5 turn off 6 eat
7 is going to

UNIT 02 미래시제의 부정문과 의문문

A 1 She will not[won't] arrive
2 Will we see Ally
3 Will the store close
4 He will not[won't] eat a hamburger
5 He is not[He isn't/He's not] going to study
6 Is she going to help
7 They are not[They aren't/They're not] going to sell
8 Is she going to get married
9 Amy will not[won't] play the piano
10 Are they going to study

B 1 Will Jim leave tomorrow?
2 Are you going to clean the room?
3 Will you answer the phone?
4 Are they going to visit the museum?
5 Are you going to go swimming?

C 1 Is, going to 2 will not 3 won't
4 Will you

UNIT 03 시제 비교

A 1 go 2 are having 3 is going 4 am taking
5 will visit 6 learned 7 visited
8 will clean 9 ate 10 is going to play
11 are playing 12 met 13 is studying
14 exercise 15 read

B 1 Do, play, play 2 Did, study, studied
3 Is, drinking 4 Will, do 5 Is, meeting

C 1 isn't sleeping 2 moved 3 started
4 O 5 isn't playing 6 danced 7 O 8 O

Grammar Test ▸▸Unit 1~3

1 I'm[I am] not going to eat chocolate.
2 Will Jimmy take pictures?
3 Are you going to come home early?
4 Dorothy will shop online.
5 Will, won't 6 Are, are 7 Will, will
8 Is, isn't 9 called 10 is studying
11 is eating 12 bought 13 gets up
14 will[is going to] leave 15 shows, show
16 Will, Is 17 met, meet
18 doesn't, didn't[did not] 19 wait, waiting
20 ①, ③, ④ 21 We had a good time.
22 He will not[won't] forget Jenny's birthday.

23 We are[We're] reading his novel.

24 He goes jogging every morning.
[Every morning he goes jogging.]

25 Are you going to learn swimming?

26 ③ 27 ② 28 ④ 29 ①

UNIT 04 can, must, may

A 1 must go 2 can swim 3 must tell
4 may[can] go

B 1 is able to 2 have to 3 can
4 are able to 5 has to

C 1 I can[am able to] teach English.
2 You must[have to] read the book.
3 You may[can] take pictures.
4 She can[is able to] make pasta.
5 He must[has to] take a break.
6 You may[can] go to the concert.

D 1 speak 2 play 3 have to 4 may
5 clean 6 to swim 7 has to

UNIT 05 조동사의 부정문

A 1 cannot 2 must not 3 don't have to
4 may not 5 isn't able to

B 1 must not wear 2 cannot understand
3 may not use 4 doesn't have to
5 must not[mustn't] 6 am not able to

C 1 may not 2 am not able to
3 am not able to 4 can't 5 isn't able to
6 cannot

D 1 don't have to 2 am not able to
3 may not 4 can't[cannot]
5 must not[mustn't]

UNIT 06 조동사의 의문문

A 1 Can 2 Do I have to 3 Can
4 Are you able to 5 Can you 6 May I

B 1 ask 2 finish 3 Are 4 Does 5 be 6 Is

C 1 Can Paul join the basketball team?
– he can't
2 May I play the computer game?
– you may
3 Can Kelly take this umbrella? – she can
4 Can Ms. Brown swim fast? – she can
5 Do they have to take a bus?
– they don't have to
6 Must I clean the room now?
– you don't have to
7 Are they able to speak French?
– they are
8 Are you able to do your homework alone?
– I am
9 Must he call his family first?
– he doesn't have to
10 Can she go outside now? – she can't

Grammar Test ▸▸Unit 4~6

1 must not 2 Can 3 don't have to
4 May 5 have to 6 am not able to
7 cook 8 has to 9 able to run 10 I go
11 fly 12 enter 13 Can 14 can't[cannot]
15 must 16 Must 17 can[may] 18 must

19 can 20 don't have to 21 can't 22 have to
23 You don't have to worry.
24 You may[can] go fishing.
25 You must not[musn't] hang up the phone.
26 I can't[cannot/am not able to] understand the movie.
27 They must[have to] keep the secret.
28 ② 29 ③ 30 ①, ③ 31 ③ 32 ④

UNIT 07 부사

A 1 ⓑ 2 ⓒ 3 ⓓ 4 ⓐ 5 ⓖ 6 ⓔ 7 ⓕ
B 1 early 2 well 3 Luckily 4 high 5 really 6 sadly 7 lately
C 1 slow 2 beautiful 3 simply 4 nice 5 softly 6 quietly 7 happily
D 1 hard 2 happily 3 slowly 4 kindly 5 quietly 6 clearly

UNIT 08 빈도부사

A 1 Peter always likes singing.
2 I never fight with my brother.
3 Jack is often late for school.
4 He sometimes takes me to the zoo.
5 They never watch TV in the evening.
6 She often goes to dance parties.
7 I can sometimes take a vacation.
8 People usually make mistakes.
9 He is always smiling.
10 Billy is sometimes kind to me.
B 1 always goes
2 never goes, always watches
3 never watches, always
4 sometimes, often 5 never
6 often watch

Grammar Test ▸▸Unit 7~8

1 loudly 2 badly 3 slowly 4 Fortunately
5 very 6 Suddenly 7 sing well
8 sometimes drink 9 eat well 10 fly fast
11 How often do 12 very hard 13 often
14 early 15 easily 16 quickly 17 late
18 quietly 19 never 20 Honestly
21 amazingly
22 Suddenly, he opened the window.
23 She always talks about other people.
24 Luckily, I took a taxi.
25 He often climbs mountains.
26 She never exercises.
27 ④ 28 ④ 29 ① 30 ② 31 ①

UNIT 09 숫자 표현

A 1 ⓔ 2 ⓒ 3 ⓓ 4 ⓐ 5 ⓑ 6 ⓕ
B 1 ten 2 twenty-second 3 three 4 first 5 thirty 6 fifty 7 twelve 8 second
C 1 two hit songs 2 my sixth diary 3 the first son 4 my second car 5 Two thirds
D 1 three 2 tenth 3 three fifths 4 the second Saturday 5 Half 6 three 7 second 8 two thirds

UNIT 10 문장의 형태

A 1 looks nice 2 tastes sweet
3 sounds beautiful 4 smells bad

B 1 Jason wore a blue cap.
2 She took a big umbrella.
3 I am going to draw a tall tree.
4 He drank a cup of coffee.

C 1 gave him a puppy / gave a puppy to him
2 bought me a new computer / bought a new computer for me
3 lent me her textbook / lent her textbook to me
4 told my sister a funny story / a funny story to my sister
5 taught me Spanish / taught Spanish to me
6 made the children a sandcastle / made a sandcastle for the children
7 sent Dan an e-mail / sent an e-mail to Dan
8 brought his brother some books / brought some books to his brother

Grammar Test ▸▸Unit 9~10

1 two thousand (and) one[two thousand oh one] 2 second 3 two fifths 4 twelfth 5 first 6 fourth 7 twenty nineteen[two thousand (and) nineteen] 8 two thirds 9 third
10 six, sixty-second
11 Will you lend me your bag?
12 She taught me English.
13 Tony gave Julia a book.
14 I ate three pieces of pizza.
15 My parents showed me a picture.
16 well → good 17 my → me
18 milk drank → drank milk
19 a sweet → sweet 20 ours → us
21 You look sad.
22 I met her on the fifth floor.
23 I ate a[one] third of the bread.
24 He lent me his sneakers.
25 She drank two glasses of orange juice.
26 Mary has a red dress. 27 ①, ③ 28 ③, ④
29 ④ 30 ④ 31 ②

MEMO

MEMO

MEMO

MEMO

GRAMMAR

BEAN

그래머빈 With Workbook

Beginning! 영어 초보자들을 배려한 쉽고 간결한 문법 설명
Easy! 쉽고 재미있는 다양한 연습 문제 수록
Active! 문법 학습을 통한 자신 있는 영어 쓰기
New! 예비중 새내기를 위한 중등 내신 대비용 문항 확충